CreativCare Services Developmental Learning Guides

Ages 3 months-5 years

Guided by Montessori Teaching Principles

Leigh Abbott, RN, BSN, MS

Follow the pathway to successful development with CreativCare Services

Disclaimer

This book is meant to provide an overall developmental checklist, as well as Montessori based Learning Guides for ages 3 months to 5 years. The checklist and activities provided are a compilation of skills that are synonymous with each age group. There are many other activities and skills that are not listed.

Please note that all children develop at different rates and you should consult your Pediatrician if there are concerns or questions about your child's development.

Copyright 2013 © Leigh Perry Abbott, RN, BSN, MS

Cover Design: Julianna Turlington

Editor: April Barnes Perry

Published by: CreativCare Services

All rights reserved. No part of this publication may be reproduced, stored in a retrieval system, or transmitted in any form or by any means, electronic, mechanical, photocopying, without the prior written permission of the publisher.

Printed in the United States of America

ISBN: 978-0-578-12284-7

CreativCare Learning Guides

Dedication

This book is dedicated to my husband Jay and daughter Ally for their love, support, and patience during the writing process. Their support has allowed me to persevere during difficult times. It is also in memory of my mother and father, who taught me strength, endurance, and that I have the ability to do anything in life. I only regret that they passed away before I completed this book.

I would also like to thank Andy and Angie Perry for their editing and overall assistance during this process.

Finally, I would like to thank my nephews, Cole Perry, Logan Perry, Austin Perry and Mason Perry, for giving me real life experiences with Child Development on a regular basis before I had the opportunity to have a child myself.

Table of Contents

Introduction 7
Chapter 1: Three to Six Months 10
   CreativCare Services Milestones (3-6 Months) 11
   CreativCare Montessori Based Learning Guide 13
   Ages: 3-6 Months 13
   Cognitive Skills 13
   Cognitive Skills Game 23
   Fine Motor Skills 28
   Fine Motor Skills Game 37
   Gross Motor Skills 43
   Gross Motor Skills Game 52
   Language Skills 58
   Language Skills Game 68
   Personal-Social Skills 74
   Personal-Social Skills Game 83
Chapter 2: Six to Twelve Months 89
   CreativCare Services Milestones (6-12 Months) 90
   CreativCare Montessori Based Learning Guide 92
   Ages: 6-12 Months 92
   Cognitive Skills 92
   Cognitive Skills Game 102
   Fine Motor Skills 108
   Fine Motor Skills Game 118

Gross Motor Skills 124

Gross Motor Skills Game 134

Language Skills 140

Language Skills Game 152

Personal-Social Skills 158

Personal-Social Skills Game 168

Chapter 3: Twelve to Eighteen Months 174

CreativCare Services Milestones (12-18 Months) 175

CreativCare Montessori Based Learning Guide 177

Ages: 12-18 Months 177

Cognitive Skills 177

Cognitive Skills Game 187

Fine Motor Skills 192

Fine Motor Skills Game 202

Gross Motor Skills 208

Gross Motor Skills Game 218

Personal-Social Skills 224

Personal-Social Skills Game 233

Language Skills 239

Language Skills Game 249

Chapter 4: Eighteen to Twenty-Four Months 255

CreativCare Services Milestones (18-24 Months) 256

CreativCare Montessori Based Learning Guide 260

Ages: 18-24 Months 260

Cognitive Skills 260

Cognitive Skills Game 272

Fine Motor Skills 278
Fine Motor Skills Game 288
Gross Motor Skills 294
Gross Motor Skills Game 305
Language Skills 311
Language Skills Game 321
Personal-Social Skills 327
Personal-Social Skills Game 337

Chapter 5: Two to Three Years 343
   CreativCare Services Milestones (2-3 Years) 344
   CreativCare Montessori Based Learning Guide 346
   Ages: 2-3 346
   Cognitive Skills 346
   Cognitive Skills Game 356
   Fine Motor Skills 362
   Fine Motor Skills Game 372
   Gross Motor Skills 379
   Gross Motor Skills Game 389
   Language Skills 395
   Language Skills Game 405
   Personal-Social Skills 412
   Personal-Social Skills Game 422

Chapter 6: Three to Five Years 428
   CreativCare Services Milestones (3-5 Years) 429
   CreativCare Montessori Based Learning Guide 432
   Ages: 3-5 Years 432

Cognitive Skills	432
Cognitive Skills Game	442
Fine Motor Skills	448
Fine Motor Skills Game	458
Gross Motor Skills	464
Gross Motor Skills Game	475
Language Skills	481
Language Skills Game	493
Personal-Social Skills	499
Personal-Social Skills Game	509
Chapter 7: Key Concepts	515
Resources	522

Introduction

The term Child Development encompasses many facets such as theoretical constructs, child safety, nutrition and developmental milestones. The milestones are derived from specific areas of development. *CreativCare Services Developmental Learning Guides* will cover the areas of Language (receptive and expressive), Fine Motor, Gross Motor, Personal-Social and Cognitive Skills. Each developmental area will include five activities and three games for a total of forty activities in each area. In addition to the activities for each age group, there will be a developmental checklist.

While the developmental checklist is a tool and a guide to use for a child's overall development, please remember that every child develops at a different rate. Never compare children and always consult your Pediatrician if there are questions or concerns.

CreativCare strives to make sure all Nannies are trained properly; education is the difference. Our model provides Nannies with the opportunity to complete Child Development training and to receive a Certificate of Training after taking an exam. CreativCare also provides additional training resources, as well as a weekly educational topic in the Nanny's Corner.

CreativCare's goal is to have educated Nannies to lead well-rounded and educated children who are prepared for Kindergarten. The achievement of our goal in turn creates an atmosphere of great satisfaction for parents. The goal will be accomplished by providing Nannies on our website with Child Development training.

Theoretical Framework: The Montessori Way

There are many different theories of child development. CreativCare's Learning Guides are based on the principles of Maria Montessori's teaching method. Maria Montessori was a Pediatric physician from Italy who incorporated teaching during her career. Maria started her interest in young children while working in an institution that had "unteachable children." Maria used her observation skills to determine the needs of the children. After a short while, Maria deducted that the problems the children had were related to the adults and their approaches environmentally with the children (Mooney, 2000).

The institution experience set the theoretical framework for Montessori's methods. The methods were perfected further when Montessori opened her own classroom. Afterward, hundreds of schools began to follow the Montessori way, which revolves around the Child-centered Environment (Mooney, 2000).

The Montessori Method includes the following:

- ❖ Child-sized furniture
- ❖ Real tools that work
- ❖ Keep materials accessible to the child and organized
- ❖ Create beauty and order in the classroom
- ❖ Compliance and Responsibility
- ❖ Schedule large blocks of open-ended time
- ❖ Observe the children

Maria Montessori believed that children should be organized, have all furnishings their size, and be provided with real life experiences. She believed children should be taught about schedules and responsibility. Montessori placed emphasis on the teacher observing the children for cues and behaviors. Finally, Maria Montessori requested that every child's schedule have large blocks of open-ended time for a child's exploration of an activity of his/her choice. The belief is that if a child is surrounded by interesting things and given the time, children are capable of great concentration (Mooney, 2000).

CreativCare's book is guided by the principles of the Montessori teaching method. The following key Montessori principles are utilized by the Learning Guides:

- Child's table and chairs; Floor mat
- Learning Basket (contains all tools and teaching items)
- Do not tell the child he did something incorrectly; redirect him and assist with the activity
- Only assist the child after asking permission
- Always allow time for exploration
- Never allow the child to be frustrated; always redirect or table the activity until another day
- Use objects and items in the child's daily environment to teach
- Create an environment that is organized and provides access to activities
- Be flexible and allow open-ended time for the child

CreativCare invites you to use the activities in this book to enhance a child's development because the difference truly is education.

Chapter 1: Three to Six Months

Infants ages three to six months are beginning to develop personalities and motor skills. They are also starting to communicate with their parents.

The top four skills for this age group are the following:

- ❖ Rolling over
- ❖ Sitting with support and without support for short periods
- ❖ Cooing and babbling; Smiling
- ❖ Visually following an object

The top four educational toys for this age group are the following:

- ❖ Infant gym
- ❖ Projection mobile with music
- ❖ Stacking toys
- ❖ Rattles

CreativCare Learning Guides

CreativCare Services Milestones (3-6 Months)

	Developmental Category	Developmental Milestones
☐	Language	Is quieted by music
☐		Responds to the sound of a bell
☐		Babble and Coos trying to imitate sounds
☐		Vocalizes to express feelings
☐		Smiles and laughs
☐		Exchanges facial expressions with parent or caregiver
☐		Listens to a conversation
☐		Turns head toward sound outside of visual range
☐	Motor	Moves object they are holding to the mouth
☐		Reaches for objects and holds them in their hands; bats at objects
☐		Rolls from back to side; turns from back to stomach
☐		Holds head steady when propped
☐		Lifts head when on stomach
☐		Discovery of object properties such as when a rattle moves it shakes
☐		Opens hands
☐		Passes object from one hand to the other

NOTE: All children develop at different rates. The above milestones are general guidelines for children's development. Some children are advanced in specific areas and behind in others. Consult your child's Pediatrician if there are questions or concerns.

CreativCare Services Milestones (3-6 Months)

	Developmental Category	Developmental Milestones
☐	Cognitive	Visually follows objects
☐		Feels and explores objects
☐		Reacts to parental facial expressions
☐		Recognizes familiar faces
☐		Responds to familiar sounds
☐		Notices contrast in colors and shapes
☐		Looks for missing objects
☐		Reacts to exaggerated sounds
☐	Personal-Social	Show awareness of their hands
☐		Wants to be picked up by familiar people
☐		Discovers their feet
☐		Smiles at a mirror
☐		Plays Peek-a-Boo
☐		Pays attention to name
☐		Quiets when picked up
☐		Laughs out loud

NOTE: All children develop at different rates. The above milestones are general guidelines for children's development. Some children are advanced in specific areas and behind in others. Consult your child's Pediatrician if there are questions or concerns.

CreativCare Montessori Based Learning Guide

Ages: 3-6 Months

Cognitive Skills

Activity: Follow Me

Goal: Develop Thinking Skills and Avenues to Learning

Supplies:

- ✓ Baby Seat, Mat or Blanket

Implementation:

Place the baby in a baby seat or lay the baby on a mat or clean blanket.

Kneel beside the baby.

Talk to the baby.

When you have the baby's attention, smile at the baby.

Watch the baby's reaction.

Slowly get up and move a few feet back from the baby.

See if the baby follows you with his eyes.

Move back to your original position beside the baby.

Slowly move to the side of the baby.

See if the baby follows you with his eyes.

A baby of this age range should be able to try to follow you with his eyes when you leave him.

Continue this process moving in different directions but always coming back to the original position.

The baby should track you wherever you go, or at least try to track you.

Cognitive Skills

Activity: Who is touching me?

Goal: Develop Thinking Skills and Avenues to Learning

Supplies:

- ✓ Baby Seat, Mat or Blanket
- ✓ Sister or Brother or Friend
- ✓ Neighbor
- ✓ Another relative

Implementation:

Place the baby in a baby seat or lay the baby on a mat or clean blanket.

Kneel beside the baby.

Talk to the baby.

When you have the baby's attention, smile at the baby.

Say the baby's name.

When mom or dad gets home, have him walk up to the baby and say the baby's name.

Next, have a less familiar person walk up to the baby and say his name.

The baby should respond differently to the caregiver, mom or dad and the neighbor.

Next, walk up to the baby and touch him on the hand.

Have the mom or dad walk up to the baby and touch him on the hand.

Next, have the neighbor walk up to the baby and touch him on the hand.

The baby should have different responses to touch and sound based on the person.

The baby should be able to differentiate between the familiar people.

Cognitive Skills

Activity: Let's Get Loud

Goal: Develop Thinking and Perceptual Skills

Supplies:

- ✓ Baby Seat, Mat or Blanket
- ✓ Toy Rattle
- ✓ Familiar Sounds (Spoon and bowl, Squeaky toy, Dog Barking)
- ✓ Unfamiliar sounds (Beep or a toy car, Musical toy)

Implementation:

Place the baby in a baby seat or lay the baby on a mat or clean blanket.

Kneel beside the baby.

Talk to the baby.

When you have the baby's attention, smile at the baby.

Talk in a soft voice to the baby and then begin to speak louder and louder.

Notice the baby's reaction.

If the baby is used to hearing his mom or caregiver prepare cereal with a bowl and spoon, bang the spoon on the bowl.

Observe if the baby is startled; bang the spoon again.

CreativCare Learning Guides

Next, pick up a favorite toy rattle and shake the rattle; do this several times.

Observe the baby's reaction.

Continue this pattern with all of the familiar sounds, including a pet barking, etc.

Next, use a sound that is not familiar to the child, such as a horn beeping.

Notice that the child is startled; this is a new sound.

Continue to introduce the unfamiliar sounds.

A baby at this age should respond to familiar sounds such as a favorite musical toy.

The next step is to alternate familiar sounds with non-familiar sounds and observe the baby's reactions to each.

Cognitive Skills

Activity: Imitate Me

Goal: Develop Thinking Skills

Supplies:

- ✓ Baby Seat, Mat or Blanket

Implementation:

Place the baby in a baby seat or lay the baby on a mat or clean blanket.

Kneel beside the baby.

Talk to the baby.

When you have the baby's attention, smile at the baby.

Watch the baby's reaction.

Make another face for the baby to see such as sadness.

Watch the baby's reaction.

Smile at the baby again, several times.

See if the baby imitates your smile.

Repeat the same procedure for sadness.

Frown at the baby and watch his reaction.

See if the baby will imitate the frown.

Continue to alternate emotional reaction faces.

If the baby is not responding or imitating your facial expressions, work on one facial expression per day.

Continue the progression through several different facial expressions.

Cognitive Skills

Activity: A World of Colors

Goal: Develop Cognitive Skills

Supplies:

- ✓ Baby Seat, Mat or Blanket; Baby's crib
- ✓ Mobile with colors of different contrast and shape
- ✓ Mobile with Black and Brown Squares

Implementation:

Make the mobiles using construction paper, wire and pipe cleaners or request that these types of mobiles are purchased.

Place the baby in a baby seat or lay the baby on a mat or clean blanket.

Bring over the mobile with different colors and shapes.

Place the mobile so the baby can see all of the colors and shapes; Do not leave the mobile alone with the baby unless this is a store bought mobile; Safety first.

Move the colored mobile around and describe the mobile to baby.

Do this several times in a day; notice the baby's reaction to the colored mobile.

Another day, place the black and brown mobile so the baby can see all of the colors and the squares; do not leave the mobile alone with the baby unless the mobile is store-bought for hanging.

Move the black and brown mobile all around describing the squares and the colors.

Repeat this activity several times in a day.

Notice the baby's reaction.

The next day, bring out both mobiles and observe the baby's reaction regarding his favorite.

Babies at this age like contrast in color and shapes.

Cognitive Skills Game

Activity: Where Did It Go?

Goal: Develop Cognitive Skills and Problem-Solving Ability

Supplies:

- ✓ Baby Seat, Mat or Blanket
- ✓ Three small toys or objects that will fit in your hand

Implementation:

Place the baby in a baby seat, lying on a mat or clean blanket.

Lie next to the baby and talk with him, describing everything that you can around the baby.

Sit in front of the baby with one of the objects in hand.

Show the baby the object and name the object.

Close your hand and ask the baby where the object is.

Put a second object in your hand and show it to the baby.

Name and describe the object.

Close your hand and ask the baby where the object is.

Repeat the same process with the third object.

An example would be a small stuffed animal.

Make sure you are showing the baby the object in your hand and describing the object.

Repeat the process again with each object daily.

The baby should start to reach out for your hand to find the object.

Let the baby touch the object each time.

Make a statement saying "there it is."

Cognitive Skills Game

Activity: Follow the Bouncing Ball

Goal: Develop Cognitive Skills and Problem-Solving Ability

Supplies:

- ✓ Baby Seat, Mat or Blanket
- ✓ Small to medium colorful ball

Implementation:

Place the baby in a baby seat, lying on a mat or clean blanket.

Kneel next to the baby and talk to the baby, getting him engaged in the conversation.

Sit in front of the baby and show him a colorful ball.

Give the baby a chance to touch and feel the ball.

Describe the beautiful colors.

Slowly start to move the ball a little near the baby.

Next, move the ball closer to the baby and further away from the baby.

Bring the ball back to center.

CreativCare Learning Guides

Cognitive Skills Game

Activity: Up and Down Goes the Sound

Goal: Develop Cognitive Skills and Perceptive Skills

Supplies:

- ✓ Baby Seat, Mat or Blanket

Implementation:

Place the baby in a baby seat, lying on a mat or clean blanket.

Kneel next to the baby and talk to the baby, getting him engaged in the conversation.

Smile at the baby while talking to him.

Vary your expressions using Happy, Sad, and Angry.

Next, pick one expression such as Happy and add a sound with the expression.

The sound should be exaggerated and be high pitched or low-pitched, not the normal voice.

Example: Smile and pretend to laugh at the baby; make the laugh high-pitched.

Notice the baby's reaction.

CreativCare Learning Guides

Next, look sad and pretend to cry; make the cry sound low-pitched.

Observe the baby's reaction; notice which sound the baby prefers.

Complete this series of directions with different facial expressions and voice pitches.

Afterward, go back and change the original pitch that you used with each emotion.

Example: When the expression was a smile and laugh, high-pitch was used; go back and use the smile and laugh with low pitch.

Complete the above directions with each facial expression and voice pitch.

Babies respond to different sounds at this age.

Fine Motor Skills

Activity: Wrist rattle

Goal: Developing Fine Motor Skills

Supplies:

- ✓ Two wrist rattles

Implementation:

Place a wrist rattle on one of the baby's wrists.

Gently shake the baby's wrist to hear the noise.

Continue to gently shake the baby's wrist just enough to hear the jingle.

Next, walk away from the baby and see if he will make the same motion with his wrist.

Walk back over and speak to the baby; see if you hear the jingle.

Allow the baby a couple of days to get used to this new sound and toy.

After the baby is more familiar with the jingle sound and the toy, take the wrist rattles off of the baby's wrist.

Take one of the rattles in your hand and present the rattle to the baby (Jingle the rattle a little).

See if the baby reaches out for the rattle.

If the baby reaches out for the rattle, let him take the rattle in his hand.

Try the same process with the other hand.

If the baby does not reach for the rattle, brush the rattle against his hand several times.

Repeat this process until the baby takes the rattle into his hand.

The baby should transfer the rattle from one hand to the next.

Fine Motor Skills

Activity: Stuffed Toy

Goal: Developing Fine Motor Skills

Supplies:

- ✓ Stuffed Toy
- ✓ Baby Seat or Blanket

Implementation:

Place the baby in a baby seat or on a clean blanket.

Sit beside the baby with a favorite stuffed toy.

Show the baby the toy in a playful fashion (Ex: Make the toy dance).

After the baby is interested in the toy, move the toy in and out away from the baby.

Hold the toy about 12 inches away from the baby.

The baby should reach out for the toy.

Continue to move the toy closer and further away several times.

Afterward, hold the toy just away from the baby's reach.

Move the toy closer and further away.

Follow the pattern of closer, further and then stop just out of the baby's reach.

Watch the baby try to reach out for the toy.

Assist the baby with taking the toy if needed.

Fine Motor Skills

Activity: Belly laugh

Goal: Developing Fine Motor Skills

Supplies:

- ✓ Baby Seat or Baby Blanket

Implementation:

Place the baby in the baby seat or on the clean baby blanket.

Sit in front of the baby.

Talk with the baby and play with his hands and feet.

Continue your conversation with the baby and the play until he is comfortable.

Next, move in closer to the baby, leading with your head.

Gently place your face on the baby's abdomen and move back and forth.

See if the baby will try to grab your hair with one or both hands.

Move your head so your hair is touching one hand of the baby's and then another.

This will encourage the baby to explore with both hands.

CreativCare Learning Guides

Continue this process until the baby uses both hands and tries to grab your hair.

If the baby seems annoyed, back away and then come back to speak to the baby again.

Play with his hands and feet.

Eventually, you will hear a large belly laugh from the baby.

Fine Motor Skills

Activity: Grasp and Release

Goal: Developing Fine Motor Skills

Supplies:

- ✓ Baby Seat or High Chair
- ✓ Cheerios

Implementation:

Place the baby in the baby seat or high-chair.

Place cheerios on the tray or baby seat.

Show the baby how to pick up a handful of cheerios and then drop the cheerios.

Repeat this process.

Monitor the baby and see if he tries to pick up the cheerios.

Take the baby's hand and assist him to grasp the cheerios, if needed.

After the baby grasps the cheerios, assist him to release.

Practice this task several times.

If the baby does not grasp the cheerios, continue to demonstrate for the baby.

You are working on the grasp and release principle.

CreativCare Learning Guides

Fine Motor Skills

Activity: Batter Up

Goal: Developing Fine Motor Skills

Supplies:

- ✓ Infant Activity Mat or Gym
- ✓ Plastic rings

Implementation:

The mat or gym should have several objects hanging down.

The objects hanging down should be at different levels.

If the objects hanging down are not varied, you can use the plastic rings that connect to alter the height.

Place the baby on an Activity mat or Infant Gym.

Do not talk to the baby at first.

Observe what the baby is doing.

Is the baby batting at the toys?

Talk to the baby and describe the toys.

Ask the baby to get the toys; say "Can you get him?", "get the elephant," etc.

Gently move the toys so the baby can watch the movement.

CreativCare Learning Guides

Continue to move the toys until the baby is interested.

Allow the baby to bat at the toys.

The baby will continue to bat at the toys and eventually reach out to grab the toys hanging from the gym.

Fine Motor Skills Game

Activity: Colorful toes

Goal: Developing Fine Motor Skills

Supplies:

- ✓ White Socks
- ✓ Colored Markers
- ✓ Colored Pom poms
- ✓ Baby Mat or Blanket

Implementation:

Take the white socks and color each toe a different color.

Take the colored pom poms and sew them on two of the toes per sock.

Place the baby on the clean baby blanket.

Place the socks on the baby and watch his reaction. Keep a close eye to make sure the pom poms do not fall off the sock and into the baby's mouth.

Raise one of the baby's feet and talk to him about the colors.

Touch one toe and describe the color while pulling on the toe slightly.

Touch the next toe and follow the same process with each toe.

Afterward, allow the baby time to explore his toes.

Observe the baby pulling on the sock and trying to get to the pom poms.

Move the baby's feet, tapping them together to strike interest if needed.

Continue to describe the colors and talk about the socks.

Fine Motor Skills Game

Activity: Texture time

Goal: Developing Fine Motor Skills

Supplies:

- ✓ White glove
- ✓ Silk, Wool, Fur, Cotton, Corduroy Swatches
- ✓ Baby Mat or Blanket
- ✓ Sewing Kit
- ✓ Velcro or Glue

Implementation:

Take the white glove and adhere via glue, velcro, or sewing each texture to a different finger on the glove.

Place the silk on the ring finger.

Place the cotton on the thumb.

Place the corduroy on the forefinger.

Place the wool on the middle finger.

Place the fur on the pinky.

Place the baby on a clean baby blanket.

Put the glove on and show the baby.

Allow the baby to explore each texture.

Next present 1 finger at a time to the baby and allow her to explore the texture.

Continue until all fingers have been touched.

Repeat the process describing each texture.

Allow the baby to explore all of the fingers again.

Which texture does the baby like the best?

CreativCare Learning Guides

Fine Motor Skills Games

Activity: Finger Tunes

Goal: Developing Fine Motor Skills

Supplies:

- ✓ Baby Blanket

Implementation:

Place the baby on a clean baby blanket on the floor.

Wiggle your fingers as you come to sit in front of her.

Continue to wiggle your fingers; the baby will like the motion.

As you wiggle your fingers, sing a children's song such as "Twinkle, Twinkle" or "Mary Had a Little Lamb."

Take the baby's hand and wiggle your fingers inside the baby's hand.

Slowly touch each of the baby's fingers.

Next, touch the baby's fingers to the rhythm of one of your favorite tunes.

Say a word with each finger touched; Ex: Touch the thumb and say "Mary had a"; touch the forefinger and say "Little Lamb."

Continue touching a finger for each important word of the song.

Repeat the process and start again with wiggling your fingers.

Wiggle your fingers into the baby's hand while singing a song.

Follow the same process above.

Gross Motor Skills

Activity: Turtle Time

Goal: Developing Head and Upper Body Control

Supplies:

- ✓ Infant Activity Mat or Gym, Baby Blanket, Floor Mat
- ✓ Favorite toy or stuffed animal

Implementation:

Place the baby on a mat or clean baby blanket on her stomach (Never leave a baby on his stomach for sleeping; always place on his back or side for sleeping).

Kneel down beside the baby and talk to the baby; this will engage her in the activity.

Get in front of the baby with one of her favorite toys.

Move the toy around and make noises to grab the baby's attention.

Next, increase the height of the toy.

Bring the toy back to the baby's level.

Increase the height of the toy and then bring the toy back to the baby's level.

CreativCare Learning Guides

Notice that the baby will start to lift up her chest and head (much like a turtle) to see the object as you increase the height.

Talk to the baby about the toy, describing everything about the toy.

Continue this process each day, strengthening the baby's muscles and head control.

If the baby starts to cry and get frustrated, stop the activity and try again later.

Some babies do not like being on his stomach. It is important to have tummy time each day for all age babies.

Gross Motor Skills

Activity: Spoon Feed Me

Goal: Using a Spoon

Supplies:

- ✓ Infant High-Chair, Bumbo Seat with tray and strap
- ✓ Spoon, Bowl and Baby Cereal

Implementation:

Place the baby in a high-chair and strap her in; if a Bumbo seat is utilized make sure it is on the floor and the baby is strapped in (do not leave the baby unattended).

Give the baby a spoon and let her play with the spoon.

Make comments about the spoon and silly sounds.

Take the spoon yourself; hold it in front of the baby.

Pretend to eat saying "yum, yum, yum."

Practice this stage for a couple of days.

The next time, complete the same process but this time place baby cereal in the spoon.

Try to feed the baby.

Do not get discouraged if she turns away or will not eat.

If the baby turns away, stop the activity for a while.

Try again later or another day.

Make sure to let the baby hold and play with the spoon first (monitor to make sure the baby does not poke the spoon into her throat).

The baby will become excited each time she sees the spoon.

Gross Motor Skills

Activity: Bouncy, Bouncy, Bounce

Goal: Developing Gross Motor Skills and Motion

Supplies:

- ✓ Nothing Required

Implementation:

Take the baby in your arms and walk around the room.

As you are walking around the room, gently bounce the baby.

Hold the baby in your arms and sway back and forth while gently bouncing.

You can say "bounce the baby, bounce the baby, here we go."

Continue this process, while supporting the head on your arm.

Afterward, sit down with the baby and place her on your lap; support the head with your hands.

Sing, "Trotty Little Horsey Down to Town, be careful little horse, don't you dare fall down."

Slowly move your legs apart and let the baby drop between your legs.

Repeat the process.

Use another song with motion.

Alternate standing and bouncing with bouncing on the lap.

Use other action songs such as "The Wheels on the Bus."

You can use this song while the baby is lying on your lap.

Do "The Wheels on the Bus" motions with the baby's legs:

> Round and Round
>
> Up and Down
>
> Move on Back
>
> Swish, Swish, Swish

Gross Motor Skills

Activity: Let's Move It

Goal: Developing Gross Motor Skills

Supplies:

- ✓ Nothing Required

Implementation:

Place the baby on a mat or clean baby blanket on his stomach (never leave a baby on her stomach for sleeping; always back or side for sleeping).

Kneel down beside the baby and talk to the baby; this will engage her in the activity.

Use this time to let the baby explore her hands, legs, arms and feet.

Move the baby's legs up and down, as well as her arms up and down.

Roll the baby gently from side to side.

Let the baby spend time on his stomach.

Switch the baby to his back for a while.

Allow the baby to explore.

Talk to the baby and show her different toys during this time period.

Babies need time to have uninterrupted exploration.

Move further away from the baby and see if she tries to come near you.

Place toys around the baby so she will try to lift his head or, if able, scoot over to the toy.

15-20 minutes of time doing these activities per day is great.

Gross Motor Skills

Activity: Bubble-time

Goal: Developing Gross Motor Skills

Supplies:

- ✓ Child's Bubbles with wand
- ✓ Infant seat, large pillows or other item to prop baby on
- ✓ Small pillows or blankets

Implementation:

Place the baby in an infant seat, or prop the baby up with large pillows all around for safety.

Wave your hands in the air, pretending to pop bubbles.

Wave the baby's hands in the air, pretending to pop bubbles.

Take the bubbles and blow them so they are high above the baby.

Show the baby how to pop the bubbles with your hands.

Blow the bubbles again and use the baby's hands to pop the bubbles.

Blow more bubbles and watch the baby try to pop the bubbles.

Demonstrate how to pop the bubbles again.

Make up a song to sing and dance around while popping the bubbles.

Gross Motor Skills Game

Activity: Action Songs

Goal: Developing Gross Motor Skills and Motion

Supplies:

- ✓ Nothing Required

Implementation:

Take the baby and lay her on the couch lengthwise.

Sit beside the baby (Never leave the baby unattended on the couch).

Sing "The Wheels on the Bus."

While singing, do the motions of the bus with the baby's legs and arms.

Start with "the wheels on the bus go round and round."

    Move the baby's legs in a bicycle motion.

Next, "the driver on the bus says move on back."

    Gently push the baby's legs inward.

"The wipers on the bus go swish, swish, swish."

    Move the baby's legs side to side (right and then left).

"The people on the bus go up and down."

>Move the baby's leg's up and down.

"The horn on the bus goes beep, beep, beep."

>Touch the baby's nose and make a beeping sound.

Make up more verses and actions and always be very animated in the actions.

CreativCare Learning Guides

Gross Motor Skills Game

Activity: Stand Up

Goal: Developing Strength and Balance

Supplies:

- ✓ Nothing Required

Implementation:

Place the baby on your lap in a sitting position.

Talk to the baby and get him engaged in your conversation.

After the baby shows interest, lift the baby up onto his legs.

Talk to the baby about how big he is standing up like a big girl or boy.

Make sure to support the baby because he cannot stand.

Bounce the baby gently on the legs; place most of the weight on your legs.

Continue and let the baby sit.

Sing a song to the baby or describe everything around him.

Lift the baby up onto his legs again.

This gives the baby a different view, as well as strengthening the muscles in his legs.

Repeat this procedure in different rooms in the house.

This will give the baby a different environment and still work with his motor skills.

Gross Motor Skills Game

Activity: The Chair

Goal: Developing Strength, Balance and Gross Motor Skills

Supplies:

- ✓ Nothing Required

Implementation:

Sit on the floor with the baby and place the baby in the middle of your lap with the baby's back to your chest.

Have some of the baby's favorite toys to each side of you.

You are acting as a chair for the baby.

The baby can reach for the toy.

Encourage the baby to use her arms and legs.

This gives the baby freedom to move, but you have control and can keep the child from getting injured.

Move the baby's legs up and down; encourage the baby to kick and move his legs.

Encourage the baby to reach for a toy with her arms.

Use this time to allow the baby the freedom to move all of his muscles.

Include music during these sessions.

This time also allows you to be close to the baby, yet provide her with independence.

Language Skills

Activity: Talk to Me

Goal: Developing Expressive and Receptive Language

Supplies:

- ✓ None required

Implementation:

Even though the baby cannot say words, talking to the baby on a regular basis is very important.

Describe everything that you can for the baby.

The baby is learning just by hearing you talk.

The baby is picking up on vowels that you are saying.

You will notice that the baby starts to vocalize while he is alone.

If you hear the baby babbling, babble back to him.

Make sure to say exactly what he is saying and add more sounds afterward.

Example:

Baby may say "Ba Ba."

You say "Ba, Ba, Ma, Ma."

CreativCare Learning Guides

When the baby is vocalizing, respond to him with statements.

Example:

"How are you today, sweet baby? You are so cute. What are you saying?

"Talk to me; Tell me all about it."

Talk to the baby while changing, dressing and feeding the baby.

Always make eye contact but when the baby looks away, you look away.

Allowing the baby to listen to calming music is also a great activity.

Language Skills

Activity: Read to Me

Goal: Developing Expressive and Receptive Language

Supplies:

- ✓ Book with Thick Pages
- ✓ Rocking Chair

Implementation:

Take the baby, get a book with thick pages and sit in the rocking chair.

Tell the baby you are going to read a story.

You should use a book with thick pages, so the baby can explore; the book will have more pictures with color.

Point out all of the objects that you see in the book.

The baby will not have the attention span to sit with you for very long.

Example: Book about animals

Describe each animal and the sound that the animal makes.

Describe all of the colors that are in the book.

Point out the objects in the picture.

Ask the baby where the kitty is; where is the kitty's ball.

Point to the correct object.

You will be surprised that one day, the baby will point to the correct picture for you.

Make reading one of your daily activities.

Language Skills

Activity: Mobile

Goal: Developing Expressive and Receptive Language

Supplies:

- ✓ Crib or Play N Pack
- ✓ Projection Mobile or Available Mobile

Implementation:

Ask the parents to get the baby a projection mobile (a regular mobile will work but the projection mobile is much more entertaining).

Place the baby in the crib for a small play session.

The projection mobile has both the hanging stuffed animals, as well as a projection feature.

NOTE: When the child is old enough to pull to stand, take the mobile portion down and use only the projection; make sure the device is secure on the crib.

Talk to the baby about what is on the mobile.

Describe each animal, their color, shape and what animal is displayed.

Afterward, turn the mobile on slowly and let the baby look at the mobile and hear him coo and talk to the animals.

Give him a few moments of this time and proceed.

The baby will watch as the mobile goes around.

The baby will talk to the mobile.

Repeat the sounds that the baby is making.

Walk out of the room and give the baby time to chat with the mobile.

The next day, start with the mobile and then add the music, nature sounds or heartbeat.

Each day, add a different sound.

After all sounds have been added, determine which sound the baby likes the best and leave on that sound.

Add the projection mobile the following day.

Follow the same process.

Language Skills

Activity: Mirror, Mirror

Goal: Developing Expressive and Receptive Language

Supplies:

- ✓ Crib or Pack N Play
- ✓ Child Safe Mirror

Implementation:

Lay the child in the crib.

Talk to the child and just have a little chat about the colors in the crib, how the child is doing, etc.

Let the baby get comfortable in the crib.

Place the Child Safe Mirror in the crib; make sure it is secure to the crib.

Show the child the mirror.

Step out of the room and listen to the baby discover her new playmate.

The baby does not realize that the face in the mirror is her own.

Walk back in the room and repeat the sounds that the baby is making.

Move the baby's arms and hands in front of the mirror.

Move the baby's legs in front of the mirror.

CreativCare Learning Guides

Continue alternating the arms and legs, commenting on all movements and talking to the baby the entire time.

Leave the room and watch the baby from a distance as he or she plays with his new friend in the mirror.

Repeat the process.

Language Skills

Activity: Listen Up

Goal: Developing Expressive and Receptive Language

Supplies:

- ✓ Blanket
- ✓ CD with Soothing Music

Implementation:

Lay a clean blanket on the floor.

Lay the baby on the blanket on his side or back.

Sit beside the baby and talk with him.

Make sounds and repeat the sounds that he is making.

Play a CD with soothing music and sounds.

Let the baby listen.

Babies are able to hear inside the womb, so he is always listening.

Having a music time on a daily basis, even as a baby is an excellent way to promote language.

You can also play some lullabies and sing the lyrics.

A great time for this learning activity is right before nap or just after the baby wakes up from his nap.

This provides a gentle, soothing, rhythmic activity.

As you continue with this activity and the baby matures, you will see the baby start to move his hands and feet with the music.

Repeat the process.

After the baby is familiar with the music, stand up and dance with the baby using slow, rhythmic motions.

The baby will love the motion and the sounds.

CreativCare Learning Guides

Language Skills Game

Activity: Finger Play

Goal: Developing Expressive and Receptive Language

Supplies:

✓ Lyrics to the song or make-up a song

Implementation:

While the baby is sitting in your lap, sing a song that involves moving your fingers up and down the baby's arm.

Ex: "Up the Path"

"This little girl goes up the path (wee, wee, wee) up the path (wee, wee, wee) up the path; this little girl goes up the path; to find her kitty (Meow, Meow)."

"This little girl runs down the path (down, down, down), down the path, down the path (down, down, down); this little girl runs down the path; to catch her running kitty."

The sillier the lyrics and the more animation you have in your voice, the better that infant will enjoy the activity.

Every time you say "up the path," your fingers are running up the baby's arm.

CreativCare Learning Guides

Every time you say "down the path," your fingers are running down the baby's arm.

When you say "wee," use a high-pitched voice and when you say "meow," use a regular voice; use a low-pitched voice with "down."

Repeat this activity several times.

Make up words to different songs.

You could use "Hickory, Dickory, Dock" with the mouse running up and down.

CreativCare Learning Guides

Language Skills Game

Activity: What is that sound?

Goal: Developing Expressive and Receptive Language

Supplies:

- ✓ 3 Rattles or objects with different sounds

Implementation:

Place a clean blanket on the floor.

Lay the baby on the blanket.

Sit next to the baby and start to chat with the baby.

Take one of the rattles and shake it near the baby (around 12 inches away) on one side.

Repeat the process on the other side.

Look at the baby's reaction.

Does the baby turn toward the side where the rattle is located?

Next, place the rattle aside and just chat with the baby.

Take the next rattle and shake it near the baby (around 12 inches away) on one side.

Repeat the process on the other side.

See the baby's response.

Does the baby turn toward the side where the rattle is located?

Next, place the rattle aside and just chat with the baby.

Repeat the process with the last rattle.

If you do not have 3 different sounding rattles, you can use any items that make 3 different sounds.

Continue this process and see that the baby will start to wait for the rattle.

If the baby does not turn toward any of the rattles, notify the parents.

Language Skills Game

Activity: Ride the Bus

Goal: Developing Expressive and Receptive Language; Gross Motor Skills

Supplies:

- ✓ Lyrics to Wheels on the Bus
- ✓ Blanket

Implementation:

Lay a clean blanket on the floor.

Lay the baby on the floor on his back or side.

Sit in front of the baby.

Tell him we are going to sing about a bus.

Sing the song through several times.

Next, take the baby's legs and move them in a wheel barrow motion to the first verse ("Wheels on the bus go round and round").

Take the baby's arms and move them back and forth ("Wipers on the bus").

Take the baby's legs and move them back ("Driver on the bus says move on back").

CreativCare Learning Guides

Take the baby's legs and move them up and down ("People on the bus go up and down").

Repeat the lyrics and movements again.

Watch the baby's reaction.

This can be completed with other songs as well.

Put motions to songs; Example: "Pat-A Cake"

Personal-Social Skills

Activity: Gaze Into My Eyes

Goal: Social Interaction

Supplies:

- ✓ None required

Implementation:

During one of the baby's alert phases; hold the baby about 12 inches away and gaze into his eyes.

Speak softly to the baby.

Move the baby closer and give a kiss on the cheek.

Gaze into the baby's eyes at the closer distance.

Move the baby away and gaze into his eyes.

If the baby turns away, stop the gaze.

The baby is trying to say leave me alone.

Give the baby time to reorganize and try again.

Continue this process several times a day.

Have a friend of someone that is less familiar try the gaze process as well.

The baby should turn away because he does not recognize the strange face.

Next, the caregiver comes back and gazes into the baby's eyes to make him feel secure again.

Personal-Social Skills

Activity:	Watching Hands

Goal:	Social Presence and Discovery

Supplies:

- ✓ Baby Mat, Floor Toy Mat or Blanket
- ✓ Stuffed toy

Implementation:

Lay the baby on her back on the mat or blanket.

Sit beside the baby.

Observe the baby's motions with her body.

The baby should look at her hands as if to try to figure out what these strange parts are that my eyes keep seeing.

Take the stuffed toy and put in front of the baby's hands; see if she tries to grab the toy.

Clap the baby's hands together several times.

Clap your hands together.

Clap the baby's hands together again.

Remove the toy and observe the baby.

See if the baby moves her hands by her eyes.

Personal-Social Skills

Activity: Emotion Motion

Goal: Discovery of Emotions

Supplies:

- ✓ Baby Mat, Floor Toy Mat or Blanket
- ✓ Child Safe Mirror

Implementation:

Lay the baby on the Floor Mat or Blanket.

Sit beside the baby.

Smile at the baby.

Observe the baby's reactions.

Walk away from the baby.

Walk back over and kneel down to the baby; observe the baby's reactions.

The baby should cry when you leave the room as he approach 5 months of age.

Observe the baby during the day for the following emotions: Anger, Happiness, Boredom.

CreativCare Learning Guides

Through observation, learn which cry or sound relates to each emotion.

Introduce a mirror and watch the happiness emotion be evoked.

Repeat the above procedures several times.

Personal-Social Skills

Activity: Feet Play

Goal: Social Presence and Discovery

Supplies:

- ✓ Baby Mat, Floor Toy Mat or Blanket
- ✓ Stuffed toy

Implementation:

Lay the baby on her back on the mat or blanket.

Sit beside the baby.

Observe the baby's motions with her body.

The baby should look at her feet as if to try to figure out what these strange parts are that my eyes keep seeing.

Take the baby's feet and pull them upward; complete a wheel motion.

Clap the baby's feet together several times.

Clap your feet together.

Clap the baby's feet together again.

Move the baby's feet up and down.

See if the baby moves her feet on her own.

Personal-Social Skills

Activity: Shades of Color

Goal: Color perception

Supplies:

- ✓ Baby Mat, Floor Toy Mat or Blanket; Infant seat
- ✓ Red object, Blue object, Yellow object, Two shades of Blue objects, Purple object, Black object, White object

Implementation:

Lay the baby on the Floor Mat or Blanket; another option is an Infant seat.

Sit beside the baby.

Talk to the baby to start the interaction.

Pick up the Red object and hold about 36 inches or so away.

Obtain the baby's attention by talking to him and holding the Red object in his line of vision; note the baby's reaction.

Next, follow the same procedure with the Black object; note the baby's reaction.

Which color does the baby prefer?

Most babies prefer primary colors at this age.

CreativCare Learning Guides

Take the two objects that are shades of blue and follow the same process of presenting one color at a time.

Notice the baby's reaction; you would think that since both objects are blue, there would be no difference.

A baby around the age of 5 months should have the ability to differentiate between shades of color.

Try again with the Purple object; observe the baby's reaction.

Follow with the Yellow object; observe the baby's reaction.

Mix and match the colors and observe which colors the baby prefers.

The baby should prefer all primary colors.

Personal-Social Skills Game

Activity: Diaper-Time Fun

Goal: Develop Sense of Fun and Music

Supplies:

- ✓ Changing table
- ✓ Clean Diaper
- ✓ Bib

Implementation:

Make diaper-time fun by thinking of games to play during this activity.

As you change the diaper, sing a song that baby likes or sing a children's song such as "Old McDonald Had a Farm."

As you lift the legs to clean thoroughly, you can motion with the baby's legs during the song.

Ex: "Old McDonald Had a Farm and on his farm there was a dog with a Ruff, Ruff here," etc. all the while moving the baby's legs up and down.

Another great game is the Peek-A-Boo game.

Take a bib or clean diaper.

Place the diaper or bib over your face and say Peek-A-Boo.

The baby will find these games pleasurable and you can continue games throughout the baby's diaper changing process at any age.

CreativCare Learning Guides

For safety, please make sure the baby is strapped down and you always have your hand on the baby. Even young babies can roll over and roll off of a changing table.

Continue the games and songs throughout the entire changing process.

CreativCare Learning Guides

Personal-Social Skills Game

Activity: Where Are We Going Now?

Goal: Develop curiosity and perception

Supplies:

- ✓ None required

Implementation:

Change the baby's environment frequently.

Changing the environment leads to curiosity and perception of his surroundings.

Remember that babies get bored just like any other age group.

Periodically during the day, pick the baby up, holding him upright (so he can see all around).

Walk him around different locations in the house.

Make sure to stop at bright colors and let the baby view the object for a few minutes.

As you stop at each object, make up a fun song to any tune you would like.

Sing the song each time you stop to see that particular object.

Develop a song for each object.

Remember that the words do not have to make sense.

An example would be the following:

Tune ("Row, Row, Row Your Boat")

"Look, look, look at the picture; the bright blue picture here; it is nice and you will like it; every single day."

The baby will associate the song as a happy experience.

Repeat this process with several other objects in the house.

At the conclusion of this activity, make sure to place the baby near something interesting such as a colorful activity mat.

Personal-Social Skills Game

Activity: Nite, Nite

Goal: Develop Sense of Trust and Warmth

Supplies:

- ✓ Rocking Chair

Implementation:

Make it a nap-time ritual to rock and sing to the baby.

Take the baby gently in your arms and sit in the rocking chair.

Start rocking slowly and looking into the baby's eyes and talking to him softly.

Tell him now we are going to sleep.

Begin to sing a soft song of anything that you would like.

Some suggestions would be:

"Rock A Bye Baby" but change the words to "Rock A Bye Baby in the Tree Tops; When the wind blows the cradle will rock; When the bow breaks (insert your name) will catch you; And always, always, be there for you."

"Jesus Loves Me"

You could also ask the parent what, if anything, was sung to the baby while in utero. Babies react to the music heard while in utero.

If not, find another lullaby or slow song that the baby responds to favorably.

The baby should relax into your arms and be content if he or she likes the activity and song.

End the activity by touching the baby's hand gently.

The baby will start to recognize that touching the hand after a song means nap-time.

CreativCare Learning Guides

Chapter 2: Six to Twelve Months

Infants at this age demonstrate gross motor skills by walking and pulling up, fine motor skills through learning the pincer grasp, language skills of saying her first word and following simple directions, and cognitive skills of locating the hidden object.

The top four skills for this age group are the following:

- Using their pincer grasp by picking up a cheerio
- Starting to walk and/or pull to stand or crawl
- Speaking first understandable word
- Following a one-step command

The top four educational toys for this age group are the following:

- Activity table
- Push/pull toys
- Stuffed animal that sings, teaches numbers and ABCs
- Ride-on toys

CreativCare Services Milestones (6-12 Months)

	Developmental Category	Developmental Milestones
☐	Language	Gives object on request when a gesture of word is used
☐		Waves Bye, Bye
☐		Responds to No, No
☐		Vocalizes using vowel and consonant combinations
☐		Indicates wants by vocalizing
☐		May say a few words
☐		Vocalizes to toys
☐		Understands names of familiar people and objects
☐	Motor	Sits without assistance; crawls and/or cruises
☐		Enjoys textures
☐		Pulls up; Can walk as early as 9 months or as late as 14 months
☐		Walks with assistance
☐		Picks up small object with pincer grasp
☐		Stacks rings
☐		Turn pages of board book
☐		Place objects inside a bowl

NOTE: All children develop at different rates. The above milestones are general guidelines for children's development. Some children are advanced in specific areas and behind in others. Consult your child's Pediatrician if there are questions or concerns.

CreativCare Learning Guides

CreativCare Services Milestones (6-12 Months)

	Developmental Category	Developmental Milestones
☐	Cognitive	Uncovers hidden toy
☐		Imitates actions
☐		Bangs objects together
☐		Puts objects inside a cup
☐		Identifies familiar pictures
☐		Pulls a string to reach the object tied to the string
☐		Drops one of two objects to receive a third
☐		Responds to simple directions and questions with a gesture or word
☐	Personal-Social	Plays Pat-a-Cake
☐		Gives affection
☐		Holds arms out to be picked up
☐		Offers a toy and releases the toy
☐		Begins using a cup
☐		Exhibits Separation Anxiety
☐		Responds to name
☐		Enjoys games with using fingers and toes

NOTE: All children develop at different rates. The above milestones are general guidelines for children's development. Some children are advanced in specific areas and behind in others. Consult your child's Pediatrician if there are questions or concerns.

CreativCare Learning Guides

CreativCare Montessori Based Learning Guide

Ages: 6-12 Months

Cognitive Skills

Activity: Object Permanence

Goal: Cognitive and Problem-Solving Enhancement

Supplies:

- ✓ Infant Seat, Floor Mat, Prop Tool or Child's Blanket
- ✓ 3-4 Favorite Toys
- ✓ Small cloth or bath cloth
- ✓ Learning Basket

Implementation:

Place the baby in an infant set, on a floor mat or child's blanket with a prop tool such as a pillow (in case the baby falls backward).

Place in the Learning Basket 3-4 small favorite toys or books and a small cloth.

Show the baby each toy one by one in the Learning Basket.

Line the toys up in a row.

Cover one of the toys.

Ask the baby "Where did it go?"; "Can you find the toy?"

Describe the toy including its color, what the toy is, etc. during this process.

Previously, the baby would move on to another toy without looking for the covered toy.

The baby should work to uncover the toy.

If the baby does not try to remove the cloth, remove the cloth and state "there is the toy; the toy was under the cloth."

Continue this process with each toy, only assisting the baby when needed.

This game can also be played by placing the toy behind your back.

The baby will move around or try to move around to locate the toy that was here but is now gone.

This skill set is helpful when looking at Separation Anxiety.

The mom or dad leave in the morning but return every day in the evening.

CreativCare Montessori Based Learning Guide

Ages: 6-12 Months

Cognitive Skills

Activity: Object Permanence

Goal: Cognitive and Problem-Solving Enhancement

Supplies:

- ✓ Infant Seat, Floor Mat, Prop Tool or Child's Blanket
- ✓ 3-4 Favorite Toys
- ✓ Small cloth or bath cloth
- ✓ Learning Basket

Implementation:

Place the baby in an infant set, on a floor mat or child's blanket with a prop tool such as a pillow (in case the baby falls backward).

Place in the Learning Basket 3-4 small favorite toys or books and a small cloth.

Show the baby each toy one by one in the Learning Basket.

Line the toys up in a row.

Cover one of the toys.

Ask the baby "Where did it go?"; "Can you find the toy?"

Describe the toy including its color, what the toy is, etc. during this process.

Previously, the baby would move on to another toy without looking for the covered toy.

The baby should work to uncover the toy.

If the baby does not try to remove the cloth, remove the cloth and state "there is the toy; the toy was under the cloth."

Continue this process with each toy, only assisting the baby when needed.

This game can also be played by placing the toy behind your back.

The baby will move around or try to move around to locate the toy that was here but is now gone.

This skill set is helpful when looking at Separation Anxiety.

The mom or dad leave in the morning but return every day in the evening.

CreativCare Learning Guides

Cognitive Skills

Activity: Strike up the Band

Goal: Cognitive and Fine Motor Enhancement

Supplies:

- ✓ Infant Seat, Floor Mat, Prop Tool or Child's Blanket
- ✓ Small Bell, Two blocks
- ✓ Learning Basket

Implementation:

Place the baby in an infant set, on a floor mat or child's blanket with a prop tool such as a pillow (in case the baby falls backward).

Place the bell and blocks in the Learning Basket.

Remove the blocks; show him and describe the blocks to the baby.

Hand the blocks to the baby and observe the baby's actions.

The baby should bang the two blocks together.

If the baby does not bang the blocks together, pick up the two blocks and demonstrate how to bang the blocks together.

You can also use other objects, such as play cups, to bang together.

Complete the same process with a small bell.

The baby should purposefully ring the bell.

If the baby does not ring the bell, demonstrate for the baby how to ring the bell.

The baby will love the sounds each object makes as they are banged together.

Another thing to try is to give the baby a block in each hand.

Afterward, present the bell to the baby; previously, the baby would probably just look at the bell, but now the baby should have the cognition to drop one of the blocks so she can pick up the bell.

Continue working with different objects and remember to describe the color, texture, and what the toy is that you are working with in each activity.

Cognitive Skills

Activity: Dance to the Music

Goal: Cognitive and Gross Motor Enhancement

Supplies:

- ✓ Children's Music CDs

Implementation:

While music promotes language, it also promotes cognitive development in infants.

Incorporate a music activity in the baby's daily routine.

Find several children's music CDs.

Tell the infant that it is music time.

Listening to children's songs daily enhances the infant's thinking skills.

To make the activity more interesting, dance around the room with the infant.

Make up silly motions that go with each song.

The infant will vocalize to the music.

Also have time for the infant to just listen to the music without the dancing activity.

During a free play time, play children's music in the background.

A daily dose of music activities and listening to music will enhance a wide range of developmental skills, including cognitive abilities.

Cognitive Skills

Activity: Walk and Learn

Goal: Cognitive, Fine and Gross Motor Enhancement

Supplies:

- ✓ Musical Walker
- ✓ Floor Mat, Prop Tool or Child's Blanket

Implementation:

One way to enhance several developmental skills is to use an Activity Musical Walker.

Bring the baby to the floor mat, child's blanket or prop tool.

Have the walker sitting in front of the baby.

Start by allowing the baby to explore the walker.

Demonstrate how to place a shape or ball into the walker and make the walker sing.

Describe all aspects of the shapes and balls, including color.

Give the baby one of the balls and see if he tries to place the ball in the correct place.

The next day, bring the walker over and stand the baby up, placing the baby's hands on each side of the walker.

Standing behind the baby, start to slowly move the musical walker forward (the walker will play a tune when moving).

Continue this process until the baby is comfortable standing behind the walker on her own.

Make sure you are always behind the baby, no matter if the infant can move on her own or not and always think of safety in the house, such as stairs, etc.

Cognitive Skills

Activity: Put It Inside

Goal: Cognitive and Fine Motor Enhancement

Supplies:

- ✓ Infant Seat, Floor Mat, Prop Tool or Child's Blanket
- ✓ Stackable colored cups
- ✓ Small block
- ✓ Learning Basket

Implementation:

Place the baby in an infant set, on a floor mat or child's blanket with a prop tool such as a pillow (in case the baby falls backward)

Place the stackable cups in the Learning basket

Take the largest cup and the smallest cup and show them to the baby

Describe the cups color and size; demonstrate that the small cup can stack on top of the large cup

Bang the two cups together to make noise

Give the two cups to the baby and let him explore the cups and all of the cups' features

Describe the color and size again

Observe the baby and see if he tries to place the small cup inside the large cup

If not, show the baby again how the two cups fit inside each other

Continue to work on this process until the baby is completing the task

Afterwards, give the baby a block in one hand and the large cup in the other hand

The baby will probably bang the two objects together and then start to explore each objects properties

Tell the baby to place the block inside the large cup; if needed, assist the baby by demonstrating how to place the block inside

The baby will eventually learn to dump the block out of the cup

Demonstrate the process as needed

Cognitive Skills Game

Activity: Pat-A-Cake

Goal: Cognitive Enhancement

Supplies:

- ✓ None Required

Implementation:

One game that everyone plays and is excellent for cognitive development is Pat-A-Cake.

There are many different versions, so pick whichever version works best for you.

Play with the baby on your lap.

Sitting in a rocking chair or regular chair, place the baby on your lap facing you.

Grasp the baby's hands and clap them together several times.

The baby should exhibit joy from the clapping motion and sound.

Continue with clapping the hands.

Next, add the words to the clapping portion.

After the baby is comfortable with the clapping portion, add the rolling portion.

Continue the same process of the clapping portion of the song, adding the rolling portion.

Finally, add the "put him in the pan" or "put him in the oven" portion.

After the baby is comfortable with each portion, continue with the song using all hand motions.

Next, observe if the baby is trying some of the motions on her own as you sing the song. (Make sure to monitor the baby carefully so he does not fall backward from your lap).

Cognitive Skills Game

Activity: Reading Recognition and Name That Picture

Goal: Cognitive, Expressive, and Receptive Language Enhancement

Supplies:

- ✓ Board Books or Books with larger pictures
- ✓ Books with pictures of everyday objects

Implementation:

Reading to your baby is a fundamental way to enhance multiple types of development. Reading can never begin too early and should definitely be increased at this age.

Have a special time every day that is reading time.

Take 2 board books and let the baby choose which book to read.

Describe everything that you can in the book.

Even at this early age, ask the baby "what is this? Is this a cat? The cat says 'meow.'"

After several sessions with the book, the baby will start to understand and try to say some of the pictures' names.

Continue this process by making or buying a large book of everyday objects (you can use the Toddler Talk Coloring Book for this activity too).

CreativCare Learning Guides

Pick out 3 specific objects or animals and concentrate on these particular objects daily.

Show the baby the picture of the object ask him later, "where is the cat?"

Describe everything about the cat or other items.

After the baby has mastered the 3 pictures, move on to 3 additional pictures.

Continue the process and the baby could be saying words at an earlier age.

Cognitive Skills Game

Activity: Walk and Learn

Goal: Cognitive, Fine, and Gross Motor Enhancement

Supplies:

- ✓ Musical Walker
- ✓ Floor Mat, Prop Tool or Child's Blanket

Implementation:

One way to enhance several developmental skills is to use an Activity Musical Walker.

Bring the baby to the floor mat, child's blanket or prop tool.

Have the walker sitting in front of the baby.

Start by allowing the baby to explore the walker.

Demonstrate how to place a shape or ball into the walker and make the walker sing.

Describe all aspects of the shapes and balls, including color.

Give the baby one of the balls and see if he tries to place the ball in the correct place.

The next day, bring the walker over and stand the baby up, placing the baby's hands on each side of the walker.

Standing behind the baby, start to slowly move the musical walker forward (the walker will play a tune when moving).

Continue this process until the baby is comfortable standing behind the walker on his own.

Make sure you are always behind the baby, no matter if the infant can move on his own or not and always think of safety in the house, such as stairs, etc.

Fine Motor Skills

Activity: Stack the Rings

Goal: Fine Motor Enhancement

Supplies:

- ✓ Infant Seat, Floor Mat, Prop Tool, or Child's Blanket
- ✓ Stackable Rings
- ✓ Learning Basket

Implementation:

Place the baby in an infant seat, on a floor mat or child's blanket with a prop tool such as a pillow (in case the baby falls backward).

Place the Stackable Rings Toy in the Learning Basket.

Take the rings and put in front of the baby.

See if the baby will dump all of the rings from the pole; if not, assist the baby with this task.

Lay out each ring and describe its color.

Pick up the largest ring and compare the ring to the smallest ring.

Hand both rings to the baby for him to bang together.

Continue comparing the size of the rings.

Demonstrate how to place the largest ring to the smallest on the pole.

Allow the baby time to explore the pole and each ring, describing the color and the size as large and small.

Demonstrate once how to stack the rings properly.

Allow the baby time to stack the rings as he would like.

Continue this process until the baby can stack the rings.

Note: It may take some time before the rings are stacked properly.

Fine Motor Skills

Activity: Turn the Page

Goal: Fine Motor Enhancement

Supplies:

- ✓ Infant Seat, Floor Mat, Prop Tool or Child's Blanket
- ✓ Cloth Books or Plastic Bath Books (Story books and ABCs)
- ✓ Learning Basket

Implementation:

Place the baby in an infant seat, on a floor mat or child's blanket with a prop tool such as a pillow (in case the baby falls backward).

Bring the Learning Basket over, containing several cloth books.

Allow the baby to explore the books and their texture.

Read the story to the baby and point out all the pictures in the book, being very descriptive.

Demonstrate turning the pages, slowly and one by one.

Hand the book to the baby and observe if he tries to turn the page of the book.

Continue with the next book, this time using the ABC Book.

Point out pictures and name the items for the baby.

CreativCare Learning Guides

Always ask the baby the name of each picture before stating the name. Ex: "What is this picture?" or "Which picture is the puppy?"

Again, allow the baby time to explore the pages of the book and see if the baby will turn the pages without assistance.

Cloth and plastic books are an excellent way for babies to work on fine motor skills before moving on to board books.

Continue this process daily.

Fine Motor Skills

Activity: Pop Up Pal

Goal: Fine Motor and Cognitive Enhancement

Supplies:

- ✓ Infant Seat, Floor Mat, Prop Tool or Child's Blanket
- ✓ Press and Pop Shape Toy
- ✓ Learning Basket

Implementation:

Place the baby in an infant seat, on a floor mat or child's blanket with a prop tool such as a pillow (in case the baby falls backward).

Place the toy in the Learning Basket and bring over to the baby.

Place the toy so the baby can reach the toy and explore.

Allow plenty of exploration time.

Afterward, demonstrate how to press, pull or turn the mechanisms to make the animal, etc. pop up.

During this time, describe the color of the button pushed, the animal or item that pops up, as well as what you are doing to make the item pop up.

Ex: "I am pushing the RED round button to make the bear pop up; I am twisting the GREEN key to make the doggie pop up."

CreativCare Learning Guides

After you demonstrate each mechanism, allow the baby to explore the toy again.

You will probably see that the baby pushes the button and only that button in the beginning.

Continue to demonstrate how to make the other items pop up on a regular basis.

Each session, begin with allowing the baby to explore and do as he wishes with the toy.

If the baby is struggling, say "may I assist?" and demonstrate how to work the remaining mechanisms.

The turning, pulling and pushing motions enhance fine motor skills, and figuring out how to turn, pull and push to reach the pop up item enhances cognitive abilities.

Fine Motor Skills

Activity: Chef Preview

Goal: Fine Motor and Cognitive Enhancement

Supplies:

- ✓ Infant Seat, Floor Mat, Prop Tool or Child's Blanket
- ✓ Large, plastic infant spoon and infant bowl
- ✓ Learning Basket

Implementation:

Place the baby in an infant seat, on a floor mat or child's blanket with a prop tool such as a pillow (in case the baby falls backward).

Place the spoon and infant bowl in the Learning Basket and bring over to the baby.

Place the spoon and bowl within the baby's reach.

Allow the baby to explore the spoon and bowl.

The baby will probably bang the spoon on the bowl.

After a period of exploration, take the bowl and spoon and place the spoon beside the bowl.

Ask the baby to pick up the spoon.

If the baby does not pick up the spoon, pick up the spoon and hand it to the baby.

Allow the baby time to play with the spoon only.

After a period of exploration, take the spoon and place it beside the bowl.

Ask the baby to put the spoon inside the bowl.

If the baby is not sure what to do, please assist and show him how to place the spoon into the bowl.

Next, allow the baby to play with the bowl and spoon as he would like.

Afterward, take the spoon and bowl away and place them beside each other.

Ask the baby again to place the spoon into the bowl.

Continue this process.

After the baby is comfortable placing the spoon in the bowl, show the baby how to stir in the empty bowl.

You are creating a mini Chef.

CreativCare Learning Guides

Fine Motor Skills

Activity: Texture Time

Goal: Fine Motor, Visual Perception and Sensory Integration Enhancement

Supplies:

- ✓ Infant Seat, Floor Mat, Prop Tool or Child's Blanket
- ✓ 6 Fabric squares of different colors, patterns and textures
- ✓ Shirt box or other box; Small Felt Board
- ✓ Learning Basket

Implementation:

Place the baby in an infant seat, on a floor mat or child's blanket with a prop tool such as a pillow (in case the baby falls backward).

Place the fabric squares in the Learning Basket and bring over to the baby.

The fabric squares should be of various colors, patterns and textures.

Hand the fabric squares to the baby one by one for exploration; allow ample time between each square.

During the exploration, provide the baby with a description of the fabric square and its pattern, as well as the texture.

Ex: "You have the black and white fuzzy square. Do you like it? It has checks" or "You have the rough, tan and orange square."

Complete this process with each square.

After you have completed the process, take two of the squares and lay them in front of the baby; tell him to get the square.

Compare and contrast which of the squares the baby is drawn to at this age.

After working on this activity, save the squares by either gluing them into a shirt box or placing them on a felt board.

This way, the baby can have the patterns to look at and touch, and you don't have to create new squares each week.

Continue this process and every few weeks, switch out that fabric for different patterns and designs.

Fine Motor Skills Game

Activity: Build it up

Goal: Fine Motor Enhancement

Supplies:

- ✓ Infant Seat, Floor Mat, Prop Tool or Child's Blanket
- ✓ Large Soft Blocks that make sounds
- ✓ Learning Basket

Implementation:

Place the baby in an infant seat, on a floor mat or child's blanket with a prop tool such as a pillow (in case the baby falls backward).

Place the soft blocks inside the Learning Basket.

Bring the learning basket over to the baby and say "we are going to play a building game."

Ask the baby what is inside the basket and then tell him they are blocks.

Place the blocks in front of the baby and allow for exploration.

Demonstrate for the baby how to place one block on top of the other, then knock the blocks down.

The blocks should have colors, textures, pictures and possibly sound that you can describe to the baby.

CreativCare Learning Guides

Place the blocks in front of the baby again and see if he tries to stack the blocks.

Describe each block that the baby picks up.

Ask the baby to place the block on top; demonstrate if needed.

Knock all of the blocks down again.

Continue working with the blocks until the baby is proficient at stacking the blocks.

Fine Motor Skills Game

Activity: Peek-A-Boo Car

Goal: Fine Motor and Cognitive Enhancement

Supplies:

- ✓ Infant Seat, Floor Mat, Prop Tool or Child's Blanket
- ✓ Empty Toilet Paper Roll
- ✓ Baby Safe Small Toy Car (Must be child friendly and have safe wheels, etc. to keep the baby from being able to swallow).
- ✓ Colored yarn
- ✓ Learning Basket

Implementation:

Place the baby in an infant seat, on a floor mat or child's blanket with a prop tool such as a pillow (in case the baby falls backward).

Take the yarn (approximately 6 inches long) and attach the yarn to the toy car.

Place all of the supplies above in the Learning Basket and bring them over to the baby.

Show the baby the little car and the string.

Place the car with the string on the floor and see if the baby will pull the string.

CreativCare Learning Guides

If not, demonstrate how to pull the string to get to the car.

Take the toilet paper roll and place the car inside the roll so the baby cannot see the car.

Ask the baby "where did the car go? Look, there is the RED string; pull the string."

If the baby will not pull the string, you pull the string and show the baby how to get the car.

Place the car inside the toilet paper roll again and ask the baby "where did the car go? Look there is the RED string; can you get the car?"

Continue this process until the baby is able to obtain the car.

You can also change the color of the yarn for a different effect, and you could attach the yarn to a different toy such as a small stuffed animal.

CreativCare Learning Guides

Fine Motor Skills Game

Activity: Pop Goes the Bead

Goal: Fine Motor and Cognitive Enhancement

Supplies:

- ✓ Infant Seat, Floor Mat, Prop Tool or Child's Blanket
- ✓ Plastic Pop Connect Beads
- ✓ Learning Basket

Implementation:

Place the baby in an infant seat, on a floor mat or child's blanket with a prop tool such as a pillow (in case the baby falls backward).

Put the pop beads into the Learning Basket.

Bring the basket over to the baby and tell him you are going to play Pop goes the bead.

Show the baby the beads all connected together and describe their color and shape.

Hand the baby the beads and allow time for exploration.

Observe if the baby tries to pull the beads apart.

If the baby does not try to pull the beads apart, demonstrate how to pop the beads apart.

CreativCare Learning Guides

Tell the baby to listen and we will take the beads apart; pop one bead from the strand.

Hand the strand back to the baby and say "you try to get the beads apart."

If the baby is still having difficulty, demonstrate again.

Make sure you are describing the texture of the beads, such as this one has ripples or ridges and the color.

Continue this process until the baby can pop the beads apart; this may take a few days.

Afterward, start the process again by showing the baby how to put the pop beads back together.

Gross Motor Skills

Activity: Moving Right Along

Goal: Gross Motor Enhancement

Supplies:

- ✓ 3 Favorite Toys

Implementation:

Make sure the floor and room are baby proof and safe.

During the latter portion of this time, babies learn to crawl and pull to stand.

If the baby has mastered sitting, place the baby on the floor in a sitting position.

Put 1 of the baby's favorite toys in front of him.

Let the baby explore the toy and play for a few minutes.

Afterward, move the toy a short distance away from the baby.

Ask the baby, "Can you get the bear? Get the bear."

The baby will most likely begin reaching for the toy and topple over; keep in mind to make sure the baby does not bump his face.

Continue this type of activity, slowly moving the toy further back so the baby will want to reach the toy.

CreativCare Learning Guides

The first phase of crawling is up on all fours rocking; the baby is not quite sure how to coordinate legs and arms to move forward.

Continue to encourage the baby to come for the toy or come to you.

After the baby has mastered crawling, place the toy onto a piece of furniture such as a couch.

Show the baby where the toy is located and encourage the baby to crawl over to the couch.

When the baby reaches the couch, if he does not pull up, assist the baby by putting him in a standing position (holding on to the couch).

Try to switch the toys to make these activities more enticing.

As discussed earlier for this age group, an activity table is great for learning to pull up.

Gross Motor Skills

Activity: Roly Poly

Goal: Gross Motor Enhancement

Supplies:

- ✓ Floor Mat, Prop Tool or Child's Blanket
- ✓ 3-4 Baby Safe Medium Balls such as Nerf, Koosh, or Soft Plastic
- ✓ Learning Basket

Implementation:

Place the baby on a floor mat or child's blanket with a prop tool such as a pillow (in case the baby falls backward).

Bring the Learning Basket over to the baby with the balls in the basket.

Allow the baby to take the balls out and explore their textures, etc.

Afterward, tell the baby that you are going to play ball.

Ask the baby to roll the ball; if the baby does not know how to roll the ball, demonstrate.

Demonstrate how to spread your legs out to receive the ball.

Talk about each ball, including size, color and texture.

Continue with the rolling process until proficient.

CreativCare Learning Guides

Next, move on to showing the baby how to hold the ball into the air and let it drop.

Assist the baby as needed.

The baby will love to see the ball drop and enjoy the entire dropping activity.

Move back and forth between rolling and dropping the ball.

Perform this activity with each ball.

Gross Motor Skills

Activity: On Your Feet

Goal: Gross Motor Enhancement

Supplies:

- ✓ Activity Walker (Optional)

Implementation:

Some babies walk as early as 9 months and some do not walk until around 14 months. If the baby is not walking by 15 months, a Pediatrician should be consulted.

To encourage walking, you can use an Activity Walker around 8 or 9 months. The walker allows the baby to have the control of standing, while pushing the walker and hearing it sing.

Place the baby on the floor and ask him if he would like to take a walk; make sure the room and floor is baby proof and safe.

Pick the baby up to a standing position; stand behind the baby and grab her hands.

Slowly start to walk forward with the baby taking one step at a time.

The baby will love her new view of the world.

Be careful not to tug or pull on the baby's arms; gently hold the baby's hands and walk with her.

CreativCare Learning Guides

Point out all of the colors, furniture and interesting things in the room.

After a few weeks of this activity, move to encouraging the baby to stand on his own and then ask the baby to come to you.

There will be falls but be sure to always catch the baby when possible and guard against him hitting her face.

Praise the baby for each step achieved.

Remember the first steps of walking are pulling to stand and letting go for short periods.

Gross Motor Skills

Activity: Peek-A-Boo Baby Crawl

Goal: Gross Motor Enhancement

Supplies:

- ✓ Store Bought Tunnel or Large Card Board Box
- ✓ Favorite toy

Implementation:

Use a store bought tunnel or create a tunnel from a large cardboard box; if you create the tunnel, cut opposite ends of the box.

Place the baby in an infant seat, on a floor mat or child's blanket with a prop tool such as a pillow (in case the baby falls backward).

Bring the tunnel out and place the baby on one end of the tunnel.

Encourage the baby to crawl through by getting on the other end of the box and calling the baby to you.

Place a favorite toy just inside the other end of the tunnel for incentive.

If the baby does not crawl through the tunnel, demonstrate how to crawl through the tunnel.

Afterward, place the baby at one end of the tunnel again and entice the baby with another toy and you on the other end of the tunnel.

If the baby still will not go through, get a ball and show the baby how the ball goes through the tunnel.

It may take the baby a few days to be comfortable with this activity.

If the baby cannot crawl yet, show her how the ball goes through the tunnel.

You can make up songs or cute lines as the baby crawls through the tunnel.

You can also play Peek-A-Boo with the baby by saying "where is the baby, where is the baby?" When he tries to crawl through, say "there you are!"

Use an exaggerated voice during these activities.

Gross Motor Skills

Activity: Over and Down

Goal: Gross Motor Enhancement

Supplies:

- ✓ Several pillows
- ✓ Favorite toys

Implementation:

Place the baby on a floor mat or child's blanket with a prop tool such as a pillow (in case the baby falls backward).

Place several fluffy pillows in different locations around the room.

Make sure the room and floor are baby proof and safe.

On the other side of each pillow, place one of the baby's favorite toys.

Tell the baby you are going to play up and down.

Encourage the baby (by getting on his or her own level) to crawl over the pillows.

If the baby does not want to crawl over, demonstrate how to crawl over the pillows.

Be very descriptive and animated when crawling over with high and low-pitched sounds.

Example: "I am going over, over, over, WHEEEE; Boom, I made it over and have my bear YAYYYYYYYYYYYYYYY"

After the baby masters crawling over the pillow, try stacking two pillows or provide other obstacles for the baby to maneuver.

Continue this process on a daily basis.

When the baby can walk well, develop additional obstacles fit for a walking baby.

Gross Motor Skills Game

Activity: Up in the Air

Goal: Gross and Fine Motor Enhancement

Supplies:

- ✓ Floor Mat, Prop Tool or Child's Blanket
- ✓ Thin Scarves; Paper towels; Ribbon
- ✓ Learning Basket

Implementation:

Place the baby on a floor mat or child's blanket with a prop tool such as a pillow (in case the baby falls backward).

Place each item in the Learning Basket and bring the basket to the baby.

Tell the baby that you are going to play a game called up in the air.

Throw one of the items in the Learning Basket up in the air.

As the item comes back down, make sure that you extend your arms to try to catch the item.

Throw the same item again and ask the baby to try to catch it.

If the baby does not extend her arms, assist the baby and extend her arms to catch the item.

Use items that float but have different colors and textures.

CreativCare Learning Guides

Be very dramatic when you throw the item into the air and make different noises.

Do the same as the item floats back down, making a different sound than when you threw the item?

Continue this game using any item that is safe and will float.

Gross Motor Skills Game

Activity: Bouncy Baby

Goal: Gross Motor and Rhythmic Motion Enhancement

Supplies:

- ✓ None Required

Implementation:

Take the baby on your lap, with the baby facing you.

Bounce the baby gently up and down saying "bouncy baby, bouncy baby."

You can put the motion to a song such as "Trotty Little Horsey."

With each verse, provide more motions and actions.

Pull your legs apart and let the baby fall between; add a high pitched sound to the activity.

Add sound to each activity.

You can turn the baby upside down, but be careful not to lose your grip or hit her head.

Try a motion where you stand the baby up and then sit him down quickly but gently.

Sway the baby from side to side.

Clap the baby's hands and feet together.

You can make up your own song or use some of the songs already available.

Make sure to repeat the same motions each day. You can always add a new motion as well.

All of the movement assists with gross motor development.

Gross Motor Skills Game

Activity: Bicycle Ride

Goal: Gross Motor Enhancement

Supplies:

- ✓ Baby floor mat or blanket

Implementation:

Place the baby on a floor mat or child's blanket with a prop tool such as a pillow (in case the baby falls backward).

Lie the baby down and lift her legs.

Move the baby's legs around and around like a bicycle.

You can make up a song or use "The Wheels on the Bus."

Afterward, you can stand the baby up and say "twist, twist, and twist."

"This is how we twist, twist, and twist."

Next, sit the baby down and say "this is how we sit, sit, sit."

Then, stand the baby up again and say "this is how we stand, stand, stand."

Add additional activities as you like and then go back to the bicycle motion.

CreativCare Learning Guides

Examples of things to add would be:

Clap, Clap, Clap

Stomp, Stomp, Stomp (holding the baby and tapping her feet on the floor)

Up and down

Be as animated as possible and use different songs.

The more the baby moves, the more the muscles develop, and these activities are fun for the baby.

Language Skills

Activity: Vocal Time

Goal: Expressive Language Enhancement

Supplies:

- ✓ Infant Seat, Floor Mat or Child's Blanket
- ✓ 3-4 Favorite Toys
- ✓ Learning Basket

Implementation:

Place the baby in an infant seat, on the floor mat or blanket.

Listen to the baby when you first place her on or in the object; the baby will coo and make sounds just from the activity of placing her in a different location.

Sit in front of the baby with the Learning Basket.

Bring out toy A and hold the toy approximately 12 inches from the baby.

Listen to the baby; the baby should vocalize to try to obtain the toy.

Previously, the baby would cry to indicate what she desires, but this has been replaced with vocalization.

Say to the baby during each process "do you want the toy? Is this what you want?"

Say to the baby "tell me about it, tell me what you want."

Give the toy to the baby and let her play with toy A for a while.

Next, take toy A away and present toy B.

Notice if the baby uses the same vocalization pattern for each toy or if there are different sounds for this toy.

Repeat the process with another toy.

This melody of sounds should be practiced and encouraged on a daily basis.

This is the baby's first try at speaking.

Language Skills

Activity: Read My Hands

Goal: Expressive Language Enhancement; Sign language

Supplies:

- ✓ Infant Seat, Floor Mat or Child's Blanket
- ✓ Everyday Activities

Implementation:

When the child is at this young age, communication is both motion, action and vocalization. Another way to teach a baby how to communicate is to use sign language; this will enhance her expressive language.

Use teachable moments, such as daily activities of eating, to teach the baby sign language .

The first word to teach the baby is "more"; tap the fingertips of each hand together.

See illustration below:

more

Tap the fingertips together; make sure the fingertips of both hands are touching each other

All during the day, each time there is an opportunity, do the following:

- ✓ Ask the child, "do you want more, more, is more what you want?"
- ✓ While saying the word "more," sign the word more as above
- ✓ This can be used at meal time, while playing games or playing with toys, and while reading a book.

Complete the above steps on an ongoing basis.

After 2-3 weeks of working on "MORE," add another word and sign.

Use the same process listed above using the different words.

"EAT"
eat / food

Move your fingers to the mouth, away and back and forth to the mouth and away quickly

"MILK"

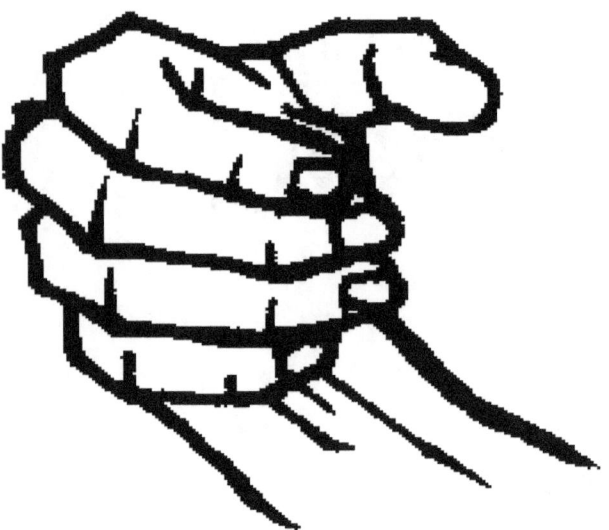

Please note you begin the sign with your hand in a C, but the next step (not pictured) is to close your hand with the thumb around the fingers, making a fist. You use both fists and bring them out into a C; the motion of making the C and then the fists is the sign.

Continue working on signs and when these are mastered, there are resources for additional signs.

Please know that signing can increase IQ and help with infant frustrations of trying to communicate.

Do not only use signing with the infant; make sure that you are using the word along with the sign.

Language Skills

Activity: Catch Phrases

Goal: Expressive Language Enhancement

Supplies:

- ✓ None Required

Implementation:

During the baby's daily activities, create key words that you use each time of the day for specific tasks. Children need repetition, and one way they try to learn words and to eventually associate words with tasks is by using the same terminology for each activity daily.

Start by looking at tasks for which specific words can be associated.

Arrival and Departure:

When mom or dad leave in the morning, always have her wave and say "bye, bye."

When mom or dad return in the evening, always have her wave and say "hello."

Mealtime:

"Time to eat breakfast"; "time to eat snack"; "time to eat lunch"

Nap:

"Time to go night-night"

Wake-up Time:

"Did you have a nice nap?"

Playtime:

Make this applicable to whatever the infant's schedule may be, such as music time, etc.

End of Day Routine:

Always say goodbye; give the infant a hug and anything else you would like to do.

Example: "Kara is going bye-bye now; See you tomorrow."

All phrases sound very general and simple, but the key is to use the same phrase each day.

Example: You can't say "Did you have a nice nap?" and then the next day say "How did you sleep?"

At this age, repetition is the key to learning.

Make your own phrases specific to your own situation but remember for certain times of the day and activities always use the same words.

Language Skills

Activity: Make a Choice

Goal: Expressive and Receptive Language Enhancement

Supplies:

- ✓ Three toys of interest
- ✓ Baby blanket; pillow or prop tool
- ✓ Learning Basket

Implementation:

Place the baby on blanket in a sitting position with a pillow or other prop tool behind the baby.

Bring the Learning Basket over with 3 toys of interest.

Place each toy around the baby.

Ask the baby to get toy A.

When the baby reaches for a toy B; state "that is a doll" (whatever the object is).

As the baby reaches for each toy, name the toy.

Continue this game using the same toys on a regular basis.

Say to the baby, "you want the doll, get the doll."

CreativCare Learning Guides

After the baby understands what each toy is and that each toy is different, gather 3 more toys or objects and play the same game.

Eventually, the baby will name the toys and items.

Language Skills

Activity: Understanding Simple Words

Goal: Receptive Language Enhancement

Supplies:

- ✓ None Required

Implementation:

Place the baby on blanket in a sitting position with a pillow or other prop tool behind the baby.

Allow the baby to crawl or move freely around the floor.

When the baby is crawling toward something dangerous, before he reaches the object, say "no."

The baby should stop at least for a few minutes and pause when hearing the word "no."

Try the same thing the next time the baby needs to be told "no," but this time say the word "stay."

The baby should not respond.

One of the first words that the baby will respond to, other than the name, is "no."

It is important to use the word "no" firmly but only when necessary.

If the child is in danger of being hurt, use the word "no."

This is the beginning of setting limits for the child.

Be sure to speak with the parent and make sure you both are on the same page regarding discipline; some parents do not believe in saying "no" to their child. If the parent does not believe in saying "no," the parent and caregiver will need to develop an alternative plan.

At this age, the baby should also recognize and start trying to say "Mama" and "Dada."

Observe the baby when the parent returns and see if she calls her parent Mama or Dada, and if not, make sure that you say "Mama is home" or "Daddy is home."

When you say any word, make sure the syllables are understandable and pronounced thoroughly.

Language Skills Game

Activity: Animal Sounds

Goal: Receptive Language, Creativity and Cognition

Supplies:

- ✓ Infant Seat
- ✓ Pictures of Animals
- ✓ Card stock or Colored Construction Paper
- ✓ Child Safe Glue
- ✓ Old Magazines, Coloring Books or Pictures Online

Implementation:

Cut pictures (from sources listed above) of basic animals such as a dog, cat, cow and sheep.

Take a piece of construction paper or cardstock and cut into 4 squares.

On each square, glue a picture of an animal.

Place the baby in the infant seat securely.

Sit in front of the child, no more than 12 inches away.

Place one of the pictures to the side of your face right by the eye. This is the appropriate position for where a child of this age will look, watching your mouth for sounds.

With the picture beside your face, state the animal's name and make the animal's sound.

Continue this process with each picture, making sure to hold the picture beside your face for a few minutes.

Afterward, hold the picture beside your face, state the animal's name and make the animal sound.

This time, wait for the child to imitate the sound you are making; say the animal sound after the child tries to imitate.

Language Skills Game

Activity: Mirror Fun

Goal: Expressive and Receptive Language Enhancement

Supplies:

- ✓ Child-Safe Mirror
- ✓ Child's blanket or play mat

Implementation:

Sit on the floor on a blanket or play mat with the baby in your lap.

Hold the Child-Safe mirror in front of you and the baby.

Give the child time to adjust to the images in the mirror.

Let her talk and play, as well as touch the mirror.

After the baby has been introduced to the mirror, point to your eyes and ask the baby to name the body part.

Continue this process with your nose, mouth, and ears.

Each time, allow the baby time to process the question before stating "this is my nose"; repeat "nose" twice, while pointing to your nose.

Work on naming body parts and playing with the mirror on a regular basis.

After the child has mastered the body parts, add additional body parts seen in the mirror, such as hair, hands, head, etc.

Continue this process until the baby is comfortable with and can name all of the body parts.

Afterward, take the mirror away and start the process again without the mirror.

The child should work up to naming all of the body parts mentioned.

The next step is for the child to name his/her own body parts.

To make the game more interesting, add the tune of your favorite baby song to the body parts (Ex: "London Bridges").

Make funny faces in the mirror.

Language Skills Game

Activity: Sing and Move

Goal: Expressive and Receptive Language Enhancement

Supplies:

- ✓ None Required

Implementation:

Even at this early age, singing songs and adding movement is an excellent way to enhance an infant's language.

Pick any song that you would like and add motions that you know.

A few motion examples are the following:

Itsy Bitsy Spider

Finger tips or both hands together starting in the lap area and moving the finger tips up until the song states "down comes the rain."

Wiggle the fingers of both hands starting at your head and moving in a downward motion until the song states "washed the spider out."

Move both hands and arms in a sweeping motion swiftly until the song states "out came the sun."

Make fists with both hands and open and close quickly; start down low and move upward toward the head until the song says "then the itsy bitsy"

Go back to the first motion above with the finger tips climbing like a spider.

Wheels on the Bus

Place your hands into a fist with knuckles facing outward; move your hands in a rolling motion until the song says "the horn on the bus."

Take your hand, palm out, and pretend you are beeping a horn with your palm until the song says "the driver on the bus says move on back."

Take both hands and make a fist; place the fists to your eyes and move the fists forward and backward, as if you were crying, until the song says "the babies on the bus."

Throw your hands in the air and then down to the ground as the people go up and down and say "the people on the bus go up and down."

Use any song or make up your own song and add motions; adding motions to the songs that you know makes the activity interesting.

Personal-Social Skills

Activity: You Can Call My Name

Goal: Personal-Social Skills and Name Recognition

Supplies:

- ✓ None required

Implementation:

It is an incredible thing when the child responds to her name for the first time. Around this developmental time is when the child will respond to her name.

To assist the child in learning her name, always use the child's name during the day as frequently as possible.

Say the child's name with every activity or interaction.

When you walk into a room, call the child's name.

When you leave the child in her crib, say her name.

Every time the child's diaper is changed, say her name.

Other suggestions are to play a game with the child and say her name during the game.

Use the child's name during each meal time.

Use the child's name during each activity.

Make sure to call the child by the name that the parent prefers.

Personal-Social Skills

Activity: You Can Have It

Goal: Personal-Social Skills

Supplies:

- ✓ 3 Infant toys
- ✓ Learning Basket
- ✓ Infant Seat, Floor Mat, Child Blanket

Implementation:

Place the infant on the floor in a sitting position or in an infant seat or on the floor mat.

Bring over the Learning Basket containing 3 of the baby's favorite toys.

Bring the toys out of the basket one by one, showing them to the baby.

Take one toy and hand it to the baby.

Ask the baby if you can see the toy.

Previously, the baby might offer the toy and then take it back.

At this age, the baby should offer the toy and release the toy.

If the baby does not release the toy, take the toy from the baby and then hand it back.

Do this several times each day until the baby learns to release the toy.

CreativCare Learning Guides

Try this with different toys and make sure one of the toys you are using is one of the baby's favorite toys.

As the activity is progressing, make sure you are describing the toy, the toy's name, color, etc.

Also, make sure to praise the baby when he/she gives you the toy.

Always give the toy back after a few minutes and say "thank you for sharing."

Personal-Social Skills

Activity: Grab It

Goal: Personal-Social and Fine Motor Skills

Supplies:

- ✓ Infant High-Chair or Bumbo Seat with Seatbelt
- ✓ Learning Basket
- ✓ Infant Cup with two handles
- ✓ Cheerios

Implementation:

Place the baby in the high-chair and make sure she is strapped in properly or use a Bumbo seat with a tray table and strap in the child.

The Learning Basket should have a bowl of cheerios and an infant cup with two handles.

Place a few cheerios in front of the baby.

Observe if the baby picks up the Cheerios.

If the baby does not pick up the Cheerio, demonstrate for the baby how to grasp the Cheerio with her pincer grasp.

Place more cheerios on the tray and observe the baby.

Continue to practice until the baby masters the finger food.

A baby this age should be able to master picking up finger foods.

The baby should also begin to use a cup during this time. The best cup to start with is a two-handled Sippy cup.

Place the cup in front of the baby on the tray.

Observe if the baby picks up the cup.

If not, demonstrate for the baby how to pick up the cup.

Place the cup back on the tray.

Observe the baby again, and if the baby does not pick up the cup, place the cup in the baby's hands.

Continue this process until the baby is comfortable with the cup.

After the baby is comfortable with the cup, put ¼ cup of water into the cup and repeat the process.

Continue to upgrade the cups as the baby gets comfortable with each cup.

A great option for the first upgrade is to use the plastic throw away Sippy cups with lids.

These cups are made to be thrown away, but they may be used over several months and then thrown away.

Personal-Social Skills

Activity: All Dressed Up

Goal: Personal-Social Skills

Supplies:

- ✓ Baby's pants and shirt

Implementation:

Use specific times during the day as teachable moments. One of the best times to teach Personal-Social Skills is during dressing. Whether you are dressing the baby for the day or changing clothes from an accident, this is an excellent time to work on dressing skills.

During the process of putting on a shirt, describe the shirt and every step you are taking to put the shirt on the baby.

To start, tell the baby "we are going to put your shirt on now; we are going to get dressed and put your shirt on."

Place the shirt over the baby's head (make sure if there are snaps or buttons that they are undone; make sure the shirt will stretch over the baby's head); use a game of peek-a-boo to get the shirt over the baby's head without too much distress.

Next, tell the baby that she will be putting her arms through the shirt.

At this age, the baby should raise one arm and then the other, to assist with putting on the shirt.

CreativCare Learning Guides

As the baby raises her arm, say "this is the right arm, where is your hand? There is your hand."

If the baby does not raise her arm, assist her with raising her arm and go through the other steps listed above.

Continue to practice with the baby on a regular basis.

Follow the same procedure for pants, socks and shoes.

When the child is older, use a dress-up doll to reiterate dressing.

Personal-Social Skills

Activity: Please Don't Go

Goal: Personal-Social Skills

Supplies:

✓ Favorite Toy and Special Toy

Implementation:

The theory about Separation Anxiety is based partially upon Erik Erikson's theory of Child Development's first stage of Trust versus Mistrust. Basically, the baby trusts the people she has bonded with and is comfortable with only those people.

Our job is to make the baby comfortable with you as a caregiver or another sitter if ever needed.

Listed below are tips to help with Separation Anxiety:

The first tip would be used when there is an introduction to a new caregiver, including a sitter. The caregiver should spend a lot of time with both the mother or Nanny and new sitter. After spending a lot of time together, the mom or Nanny should slowly start going into another room only for a few minutes and leave the baby alone with the new caregiver. Next, the mom should start leaving her home for only a few minutes and returning. This should continue over a span of a few weeks, each time increasing the time that mom or the Nanny is away from the baby.

Before the mom or Nanny leaves the baby, make sure the following is happening:

1. Always make sure there is a favorite toy or something consistent that will be with the baby when you leave.
2. Always tell the baby goodbye, give her a kiss and tell her you will be back soon.
3. Do not make a big deal out of leaving or cling on with a long hug, etc. Give a quick hug and kiss and say "I will see you just a little later (say the baby's name)."
4. The caregiver should know which toys are baby's favorites and try to distract with the toys or by singing a favorite song.
5. The caregiver should have something that is unique to her as well, such as a song, toy, etc., so the baby will associate the activity or toy to pleasure with the caregiver.

One of the biggest things to know is it is ok for the baby to cry some. If the baby is crying the entire time the parents are gone, it may be an issue with the new caregiver not knowing how to console a baby and training may be necessary. It is ok if the baby is crying when the parents leave, and the baby might cry when he they return as well. It is very important that the mom or Nanny does not show worry or too much emotion when leaving the baby. Although it is excruciating, it is important because the baby knows enough about emotion at this age to know when her mom or Nanny is anxious or upset.

Personal-Social Skills Game

Activity: Bigger Than the Sky

Goal: Personal-Social Skills

Supplies:

- ✓ Child's Blanket, Infant Seat or Play Floor mat

Implementation:

Sit on the floor with the baby in a sitting position.

Ask the baby "how big is (state the baby's name)?"

Reply with "SOOOO Very Big, Even Bigger Than the Sky," while holding up the baby's arms.

Continue this process on a regular basis.

Make sure to use the same words each time until the baby understands the game fully.

Repetition is very important in developing the baby's understanding.

You will know that the baby has an understanding when she holds her arms up by herself and smile at the caregiver saying "SOOOOOOO Big, Even Bigger Than the Sky."

After the baby has an understanding of this game, change up the game and ask the baby additional questions with different motions.

An example might be: "How Happy is (state baby's name)?"

The reply will be "SOOOOOOOOOOO Very Happy," while smiling at the baby and clapping her hands together.

Another example might be: "How Sweet is (state baby's name)?"

The reply will be "SOOOOOOOOOOO Very Sweet Just Like Candy," while giving the baby hugs.

Continue developing creative games and work with the baby on a regular basis.

CreativCare Learning Guides

Personal-Social Skills Game

Activity: Social Hour

Goal: Personal-Social Skills and Environmental Adjustment

Supplies:

- ✓ None required

Implementation:

Before beginning this activity, it is important to speak with the parents about the neighborhood and neighbors. If the neighborhood is not as safe as you would like or the neighbors are strangers, find another location for this activity with the parents' assistance.

On a nice day, take the baby for a walk around the neighborhood or to the neighborhood park.

Use this time to describe everything you can to the baby, such as cars, trees, a dog, a cat, etc. Be as descriptive as you can.

While on this walk, interact with people in the neighborhood.

Introduce the people with whom you are interacting to the baby.

The baby will not understand everything, but this is the beginning of introducing the baby to socialization.

Other ideas for socialization include the library at story time, Gymboree classes or similar places (the mall, a park, children's museum, play dates).

The more that the baby is exposed to the outside world, the better the baby will be able to adapt when he is placed in a school setting.

The more interaction the baby has with other people, the better her social and emotional development.

Personal-Social Skills Game

Activity: Touch Your Fingers

Goal: Personal-Social Skills

Supplies:

- ✓ None noted

Implementation:

Touch is very important to the development of a baby's senses.

Use every opportunity during the day, such as diaper changes, mealtime, story time, etc., to touch the infant and bond.

Just as mom bonds with the baby, the Nanny bonds too.

Get the baby used to different body parts, such as hands, fingers, toes, arms, legs, face and head, being touched during the day.

Play games and sing songs touching the baby's nose, cheeks, fingertips and toes etc.

An example of a song could be "Head, Shoulders, Knees and Toes" or you can make up your own song.

Have an activity of rocking the baby, while cuddling her and stroking the hair or rubbing the baby's back.

Touch is vital to infant bonding. It also helps the baby when the doctor needs to examine her; the baby is used to being touched on her fingers and toes.

Incorporating a cuddling and quiet time into the baby's routine is essential.

Bonding time can also be while playing a game.

You can hug the baby, while praising her for clapping her hands or saying a word.

Everything you can do to use touch during the day is very beneficial to the development of a well-rounded child.

Chapter 3: Twelve to Eighteen Months

Infants at this age demonstrate gross motor skills of walking well, fine motor skills of turning pages of a book, language skills of giving objects upon request and imitating sounds, and cognitive skills of recognizing the circle.

The top four skills for this age group are the following:

- Using their pincer grasp by picking up a cheerio
- Starting to walk and/or pull to stand or crawl
- Speaking first understandable word
- Follow a one-step command

The top four educational toys for this age group are the following:

- Activity table
- Push/pull toys
- Stuffed animal that sings, teaches numbers and ABCs
- Ride-on toy

CreativCare Learning Guides

CreativCare Services Milestones (12-18 Months)

	Developmental Category	Developmental Milestones
☐	Language	Says at least 5 words spontaneously; verbally labels 2 or more objects on request
☐		Imitates animal sounds
☐		Says "Thank you"
☐		Gives 3 objects on request
☐		Responds to simple commands
☐		Points to 3 body parts
☐		Makes up their own language
☐		Imitates vocal sounds by an adult
☐	Motor	Walks alone by or before 15 months
☐		Throws a ball
☐		Uses a spoon
☐		Stacks 2 to 3 small blocks
☐		Places round circle in a puzzle
☐		Scribbles
☐		Picks up small objects
☐		Pushes and pulls objects

NOTE: All children develop at different rates. The above milestones are general guidelines for children's development. Some children are advanced in specific areas and behind in others. Consult your child's Pediatrician if there are questions or concerns.

CreativCare Services Milestones (12-18 Months)

	Developmental Category	Developmental Milestones
☐	Cognitive	Imitates motions such as stirring
☐		Unwraps hidden object
☐		Places a round shape in a form board
☐		Places objects in a container and dumps the objects
☐		Matches colored objects
☐		Distinguishes different sounds each object makes
☐		Identifies familiar objects in story books
☐		Show imagination in pretend play
☐	Personal-Social	Initiates social contact with peers but plays by herself (parallel play)
☐		Holds cup with two hands
☐		Removes shoes and socks
☐		Recognizes herself in a mirror
☐		Show intense feelings for their parents and affection for others
☐		Imitates another child at play
☐		Repeats a performance when laughed at
☐		Waits for needs to be met

NOTE: All children develop at different rates. The above milestones are general guidelines for children's development. Some children are advanced in specific areas and behind in others. Consult your child's Pediatrician if there are questions or concerns.

CreativCare Learning Guides

CreativCare Montessori Based Learning Guide

Ages: 12-18 Months

Cognitive Skills

Activity: Present for Me

Goal: Increase Cognitive and Problem-Solving Skills

Supplies:

- ✓ Small toy
- ✓ Wrapping paper
- ✓ Paper bag
- ✓ Learning Basket
- ✓ Child's Small Table and Chairs

Implementation:

Bring the child over to the small table.

The table should have the Learning Basket with wrapping paper, a paper bag and a small toy inside.

Tell the child that today you will find the surprise located in the wrapping paper.

Quickly wrap the toy inside the wrapping paper without tape or accuracy.

Present the wrapped toy to the child.

Ask the child to find the toy.

Give the child ample time to try to locate the toy.

If the child is having difficulty, ask if you can assist by unwrapping one corner of the paper.

Place the paper back in front of the child and see if the child can locate the toy.

If the child is still having difficulty, go ahead and unwrap the toy with the child.

Next, wrap the toy again and let the child try again.

If the child is having no difficulty, wrap different objects to see if he can problem-solve and figure out how to get the toy.

After using the wrapping paper, try the same process with a bag.

Never leave the child alone with a paper bag for safety concerns about the child putting the bag over her head.

Cognitive Skills

Activity: Match it up

Goal: Increase Cognitive Skills and Color Skills

Supplies:

- ✓ Socks of different colors
- ✓ Couch or chair
- ✓ Learning Basket
- ✓ Child's Small Table and Chairs

Implementation:

Place colored socks in the Learning Basket.

Ask the child to join you at the table with the Learning Basket.

Tell her you are going to match colors.

Place a red, blue, green or yellow sock on the table in front of the child.

Pull a red, blue, green or yellow sock from the Learning Basket.

Afterward, ask the child to place the sock from the Learning Basket with its match.

Tell the child to find the sock that looks just like the red one, etc.

Continue this process with each color sock.

Next, place all of the colors of socks out on the table.

See if the child can pick the correct sock from the Learning Basket to match the socks on the table.

This activity not only enhances cognitive skills but also promotes learning to help with chores at an early age, which fosters responsibility.

Cognitive Skills

Activity: Pull the String

Goal: Increase Cognitive Skills and Problem-Solving Ability

Supplies:

- ✓ Colored yarn
- ✓ Small stuffed animal or item

Implementation:

One way to work on problem-solving with this age group is to teach that actions lead to results.

Take a piece of colored yarn (make sure that the yarn is not long enough to wrap around the child's neck).

Tie a small stuffed animal or item to the end of the string.

Place the tied animal or item in a straight line on the floor.

Bring the child over to the area and have the child sit down.

Show her the string with the animal.

The child should reason that if she pulls the string, she can get the animal or item.

If the child tries to reach for the animal instead of pulling the string, intervene and ask if you may assist.

Demonstrate for the child how to pull the string to obtain the object.

Continue this process until mastered.

Try this process with a string and another object, following the same steps.

Another idea is to place an object of interest to the child on the floor and place a box in front of the object.

At this age, the child should have the cognitive ability to reason that if she reaches around or over the box or move the box, she can obtain the object.

Follow the same series of actions as listed above, intervening only if needed.

Cognitive Skills

Activity: Guess What Is Inside

Goal: Increase Cognitive Skills and Problem-Solving Ability

Supplies:

- ✓ Stackable boxes of different sizes
- ✓ Special toy treat, such as small book or stuffed animal

Implementation:

Stack all of the boxes inside of each other with the smallest box on the bottom.

Make sure the boxes vary in size greatly.

Under the last box, place a special prize such as a small board book or small stuffed animal.

Bring the child into the room and show the child the boxes.

Ask the child what is inside the box.

As the child gets to another box, tell her there is another box.

Ask the child "What is inside the next box?"

Continue with the process.

Try to build the excitement with each box that is uncovered.

Make sure that the child is not getting too frustrated.

If the child is getting frustrated, ask if you can assist her.

The child will be very surprised when he reaches the final box and it contains a special prize.

You can alter this activity by placing a surprise in additional boxes.

Another variation would be to place the boxes around the room and let the child uncover the surprise.

Cognitive Skills

Activity: Which One?

Goal: Increase Cognitive Skills and Discovery

Supplies:

- ✓ 4 objects that make noise (make sure the noise is not too loud for the child's ears)
- ✓ Cloth to cover noise makers

Implementation:

Place 4 types of noise makers on the floor.

Ex: 2 different rattles, buzzer and bell

Cover all noise makers with a large cloth.

Bring the child to the room and have her sit in front of the noise makers.

Uncover the noise makers.

Take each noise maker in front of the child and make the noise.

Cover all noise makers again.

Slightly uncover one of the noise makers and make the noise.

Cover all noise makers again.

CreativCare Learning Guides

Next, uncover all noise makers and ask the child to choose which one is making the noise.

If the child is unsure, make the noise of each noise maker again, asking the child to listen carefully.

Follow the entire process listed above again.

If the child continues to have difficulty, consider removing one of the noise makers.

Next, follow the same process again.

Continue to work on the process until mastered.

Cognitive Skills Game

Activity: Follow the Leader

Goal: Increase Cognitive Skills

Supplies:

✓ None Required

Implementation:

The child should be able to follow simple commands, and one way to assess that skill is by playing a simple game of Follow the Leader.

Start by bringing the child to the middle of the room and sit down on the floor with the child.

Begin with a simple command of patting the floor.

Pat your hand on the floor gently.

See if the child will automatically pat her hand on the floor.

If the child does not follow, demonstrate again.

If the child still does not follow the direction, slowly take the child's hand and pat the floor gently.

Continue to repeat the process of demonstrating and actually taking the child's hand if needed.

After this skill is mastered, try additional actions that are slightly more difficult.

Try the above directions using pat your head.

Continue the process until the skill is mastered.

Move to a more coordinated skill of clapping your hands.

Continue the process until the skill is mastered.

Add another skill of touching your nose.

Continue the process until the skill is mastered.

Add directions as you wish, but remember only to add single commands for the child to follow.

Cognitive Skills Game

Activity: Toys to Explore

Goal: Increase Cognitive Skills and Imagination

Supplies:

- ✓ Fisher Price Little People or similar house
- ✓ Fisher Price Laugh and Learn toys or similar such as mower or kitchen

Implementation:

Activities do not always have to be completed with made or created items. Toys are a very important aspect in the child's development.

Make sure to encourage the parents to have appropriate toys for each stage of the child's development.

The Little People house (or something similar) can inspire creativity and cognition.

Using the Little People house as an example, see below:

The house has a number of unique features such as

- ➢ Doorbell
- ➢ Flushing Toilet
- ➢ Upstairs and Downstairs
- ➢ Washer with sound
- ➢ Phone with sound

All of these features provide a great environment for enhancing cognitive skills.

Let the child explore the features by himself.

Afterward, show the child specific features while pretending to use the phone or wash clothes.

Another great learning toy is the push mower, which has the following features:

- Sings A,B, C's
- Pretend mower sound
- Asks the child questions

There are multiple other toys by different companies that enhance learning and problem-solving skills.

Cognitive Skills Game

Activity: Toddler Home

Goal: Increase Cognitive Skills and Imagination

Supplies:

- ✓ Child's table and chairs
- ✓ Sheet or large blanket
- ✓ Small flashlight

Implementation:

Take the child's table (remove all chairs) that is normally used for activities and cover the table with a cloth or blanket.

Place a flashlight underneath the table. Invite the child to join you under the table.

Tell the child this is a house and you can bring friends, animals or whatever he likes into the house.

Give the child a chance to get used to the house. After the child is comfortable, leave the child with the house to explore and play.

If the child is not comfortable, it is fine for the caregiver to stay in the house with the child. Encourage the child to bring stuffed animal friends or figures into the house.

This is an excellent way to ignite the child's imagination and creativity.

Fine Motor Skills

Activity: Build It

Goal: Increase Fine Motor Skills

Supplies:

- ✓ Wooden ABC Blocks
- ✓ Plastic Cups
- ✓ Small Jewelry Boxes
- ✓ Child's Small Table and Chairs
- ✓ Learning Basket

Implementation:

Ask the child to go to the small table and have a seat.

Bring over the Learning Basket and ask the child what is in the box.

If the child does not know, tell him blocks are in the basket.

Demonstrate once how to stack 2 blocks; describe everything that you can about the blocks (color, letter, and picture).

Ask the child to stack 2 blocks.

If the child has difficulty, ask him if you may assist.

If the child is able to stack the blocks, even if they are not stacked perfectly, let this stand as a success.

If the child cannot stack the blocks, continue to work with him on a daily basis.

If the child can stack the blocks, ask the child to stack 3 blocks (describe color, letter and picture).

If the child is not able to stack the blocks, demonstrate and then have the child try again.

Continue this process with 4 blocks (describe color, letter and picture).

Work on this process daily until mastered.

Other ideas would be to use small jewelry cardboard boxes or colored stackable plastic cups.

Fine Motor Skills

Activity: Round It Up

Goal: Increase Fine Motor and Cognitive Skills

Supplies:

- ✓ 2-3 Piece Puzzle Made of Shapes
- ✓ Child's Small Table and Chairs
- ✓ Learning Basket

Implementation:

Ask the child to go to the small table and have a seat.

Bring over the Learning Basket and ask the child what is in the box.

Show the child the puzzle and describe all aspects of the puzzle.

Example: "See the puzzle with shapes; here is the circle and the circle is round; here is the square with 4 sides; here is the triangle with 3 sides."

Take the puzzle shapes and place them out on the table side by side.

Point to the shapes on the puzzle board.

Ask the child to place the circle in the correct place on the puzzle board.

If the child struggles, ask if you may assist.

Place the circle in the correct location; next, place another shape and then the third shape.

Afterward, tell the child to dump the puzzle pieces out onto the table.

Assist the child if needed.

Line the puzzle pieces up again side by side.

Ask the child to put the round piece in the board.

Make sure to teach him about puzzles and how you try one place and if it doesn't fit, move the piece around. If it still doesn't fit; try another area.

Fine Motor Skills

Activity: Color Me Happy

Goal: Increase Fine Motor Skills and Creativity

Supplies:

- ✓ Child's Small Table and Chairs
- ✓ Coloring Book
- ✓ Crayola Crayons
- ✓ Learning Basket

Implementation:

Ask the child to join you at the table.

Bring over the Learning Basket containing a coloring book and crayons.

Tell the child you will be coloring a picture.

Allow the child to choose which picture he would like to color.

Allow the child to choose 1-2 crayons.

Describe the colors of the crayons and the picture that was chosen.

Step back and see what the child does with the crayon.

If he is unsure what to do, demonstrate for him how to color.

When you demonstrate, make sure to color within the lines. Even though a child of this age does not have that capability, always show him the correct way.

Fine Motor Skills

Activity: Use a Spoon

Goal: Increase Fine Motor Skills

Supplies:

- ✓ Infant Rubber Spoon
- ✓ Cheerios
- ✓ Infant Bowl
- ✓ High-chair

Implementation:

Place the child in her high-chair.

Add cheerios to the baby's bowl.

Hand the child the rubber spoon.

Allow the child to play with the spoon and become accustomed to feel of the spoon on her gums.

Next, demonstrate how to use the spoon and scoop up the Cheerios.

Afterward, place the spoon in the Cheerios and allow the baby to try.

Watch the child carefully and let him play with the Cheerios at will.

If the child is struggling and getting frustrated, ask if you can help and demonstrate again if needed.

CreativCare Learning Guides

Continue to work on this process. Once the child has mastered the Cheerios, move to additional substances such as pudding.

Start to give the child the spoon to use during each meal.

Fine Motor Skills

Activity: Turn the Page

Goal: Increase Fine Motor and Expressive Language Skills

Supplies:

- ✓ Chunky Books or Board Books
- ✓ Children's Book
- ✓ Rocking Chair or Comfortable Chair
- ✓ Learning Basket

Implementation:

Tell the child it is story time and sit him in your lap, while sitting in a comfortable chair or rocking chair.

Read a board book or chunky book and offer to let the child turn the pages.

Afterward, read a regular-sized children's book and offer to let the child turn the pages.

Repeat at story time every day.

Next, have the child join you in the middle of the floor.

Bring over the Learning Basket, which contains board books and other books.

Take one of board books out of the Learning Basket.

Place the book beside the child and ask him to look at the book.

If the child is not turning the pages, ask if you can assist.

After a few days with the board books, take one of the regular-sized books out of basket and ask the child to look at the book.

The child should be turning groups of pages. If he is turning the pages one by one, that is even better.

Allow the child time to explore the book alone.

Afterward, sit with the child and describe the page of the book, even if not sequential pages.

Observe. The more you do this activity, the more expressive language you will hear.

The child will start to develop her own "reading" language.

Fine Motor Skills Game

Activity: Little Artist

Goal: Increase Fine Motor Skills

Supplies:

- ✓ Coloring Book or Paper
- ✓ Child's Small Table and Chairs
- ✓ Artist Smock
- ✓ Learning Basket

Implementation:

Place all items in the Learning Basket and bring the basket to the table and chairs.

Ask the child to join you at the table.

Tell the child she can draw or color anything she would like.

Allow time for the child to explore with the crayons and coloring book, or to draw on plain paper.

If the child is unsure how to proceed, show the child how to draw a circle or line.

Afterward, place the paper and crayons in front of the child again and back away.

Praise the child for her efforts and describe the picture or mark that the child created.

Try the activity with washable paint or markers.

You could also use chocolate pudding to paint.

This activity is used to allow the child to start to have freedom of expression.

Fine Motor Skills Game

Activity: Cheerio Game

Goal: Increase Pincer Grasp and Cognitive Skills

Supplies:

- ✓ Cheerios Book
- ✓ Cheerios
- ✓ Learning Basket
- ✓ Snack container
- ✓ Child's Small Table and Chairs

Implementation:

Place a handful of Cheerios in a snack container.

Take the snack container and the Cheerios book and place in the Learning Basket

Ask the child to join you at the table.

Place 3 Cheerios on the table.

Ask the child to place the Cheerios back into the container.

If the child completes this task without difficulty, move to the next step.

If the child has difficulty, demonstrate how to move the Cheerios back into the container.

CreativCare Learning Guides

Move forward with the next portion of the activity after the picking up and moving the Cheerios is complete.

Pull the Cheerios book out of the Learning Basket.

Review the pages of the Cheerios book.

Next, demonstrate on the first page how to place a Cheerio.

Read the book and ask the child to place the Cheerio where shown.

Make the game fun by letting the child place one Cheerio and eat one Cheerio.

It may take several tries to get the Cheerio into the correct location.

Continue to practice with the book and with picking up small objects in general. Make sure to always have safety in mind when you pick out the object and never leave the child alone.

Fine Motor Skills Game

Activity: Shape Exploration

Goal: Increase Fine Motor and Cognitive Skills

Supplies:

- ✓ Old Shoe Box
- ✓ Poster Board Knife
- ✓ Learning Basket
- ✓ Child's Small Table and Chairs

Implementation:

Take an old shoe box lid; use the poster board knife to cut shapes of a circle, square and triangle (for simplicity, use shapes from other puzzles or games as a template to cut the box top).

Save the cut-out shapes.

Ask the child to join you at the table.

Bring over the Learning Basket with the box and shapes.

Show the child that he can store toys, etc. in the shoe box.

Next, show the child that the box with toys can become a puzzle.

Place the lid on the box and put the circle in the correct cutout.

Show the child that the shape then goes into the box.

Repeat the process with each shape.

Afterward, take all of the shapes and place them to the side.

Place the box with the lid attached in front of the child and move the shapes beside the box.

Ask the child to place the circle shape into the box.

Repeat with the other shapes.

Next, start the process again but this time wait to see what the child will do without your direction.

Continue to work with the box and shapes.

Another option would be to cut out other things in the box lid, such as ABC's.

Make sure not to cut out more than 3 of the chosen item.

Gross Motor Skills

Activity: Take a Stroll

Goal: Increase Gross Motor Skills and Receptive Language

Supplies:

- ✓ Favorite Toy or Object

Implementation:

Bring one of the child's favorite toy cars, dolls or stuffed animals and place the item on the floor near the center of the room.

Bring the child to the center of the room.

Sit down with the child.

Stand the child up while holding him around the waist.

Slowly let the child go if she can stand on her own.

Show the child where the toy is located (the toy should be no more than a few feet away from where the child was sitting).

Ask the child to get the toy. Use exciting phrases, such as "Can you get it? The bear would like to play with you."

Continue this activity, moving the toys in different locations.

Encourage the child to go after the object.

Do not let him get too frustrated; instead, give the child the object and try again later.

Try this activity in multiple rooms in the house; make sure the room is safe for the child by removing all potential safety concerns from the room.

Note: If a child is not walking on her own by 15 months of age, suggest to the parent that they may wish to speak with her Pediatrician.

Encourage walking by taking the child's hand and walking around the house or in the yard.

Gross Motor Skills

Activity: Fun with Boxes

Goal: Increase Gross Motor Skills

Supplies:

- ✓ Open Card Board Box
- ✓ Favorite Toys or Objects

Implementation:

Place an open medium to large cardboard box in the middle of the room.

Place a few of the child's favorite toys around the room.

Bring the child over or request that the child come over and see what is in the box.

Nothing is in the box; describe and show the child that nothing is in the box.

Grab one of the child's toys and throw the toy into the empty box.

Show the child that the toy is in the box.

Ask what other toys the child might like to live in the box.

Encourage the child to go and get the toy to place the toy into the box.

Continue with this game.

Dump all the toys from the box.

Leave out the toys and the empty box and observe the child.

Encourage the child to explore the box.

See if the child attempts to climb into the box.

If the child does not attempt to climb into the box, place the child playfully into the box and then bring her out of the box.

Continue this process until the child is more familiar with the box.

Afterward, give the child some space and see how she explores the box.

Soon, the child will be using her skills to climb in and out of the box.

Gross Motor Skills

Activity: Play Ball

Goal: Increase Gross Motor Skills

Supplies:

- ✓ Medium ball (Ex: Nerf ball or soft ball); large plastic ball
- ✓ Learning Basket

Implementation:

Place the child in the center of the room.

Bring over the Learning Basket with the ball inside the basket.

Ask the child what is in the basket.

Describe the ball to the child (round, color, feel) and repeat the word "ball" every chance possible.

Take the ball out of the basket.

Place the ball back into the basket and ask the child to get the ball.

If the child does not take the ball, bring the ball out of the basket again.

Roll the ball gently across the floor.

Ask the child to roll the ball.

Continue to practice until the child is rolling the ball.

Later, take the child outside to a safe area or an indoor playroom and show him how to throw the ball.

Place the ball beside the child and see if he will throw the ball on his own.

Continue to work with the child until he is throwing the ball.

As the child masters throwing and rolling the ball, start to work with him on catching the ball.

Show the child how to cup his hands and arms to catch a large ball.

Gross Motor Skills

Activity: Up and Down

Goal: Increase Gross Motor Skills

Supplies:

- ✓ Play stairs; outside stairs; stairs to slides; indoor stairs
- ✓ Picture of stairs and children climbing
- ✓ Child's stuffed animal or doll

Implementation:

Whatever type of stairs that you choose, make sure you are only working with about 3 stairs.

Safety: After you begin this exercise, the child will start to try to master the stairs on her own. Never leave a child unattended with stairs.

As the child learns to walk well, he will begin to try to climb.

An important gross motor skill is the art of climbing and maneuvering stairs safely.

Start showing the child a picture or reading a book where a person climbs stairs.

Talk about stairs and how he goes up and down.

Take the child and her doll to a set of stairs.

Allow the doll to go up and down; continue this process.

Afterward, take the child's hand and show him how to step up one stair; say we are going "up, up, up."

Next, help the child step down; say we are going "down, down, down."

Continue with the process; as the child gets older, he will learn to master walking up and down stairs.

If there are no outside stairs, take the child to a park or other area.

Practice on different stairs.

Gross Motor Skills

Activity: VROOM, VROOM

Goal: Increase Gross Motor Skills

Supplies:

- ✓ Ride-on Toy

Implementation:

Tell the child you are going to pretend to drive a car or train (whatever the toy is, use that name).

Take the child over to the ride-on toy and show him the toy.

Describe the toy including color and function; make the sound "VROOM, VROOM."

Place the child on the ride toy and let him get used to the feel of the toy.

Talk to the child, telling him all about the toy and describing everything possible.

Slowly start moving the ride while holding on to the child.

Continue to push the child if he seems fine.

Make the "VROOM, VROOM" sound.

Bring the ride-on toy back to a stand-still.

Take the child off the toy.

Watch the child and see if he tries to get on the ride-on toy.

Encourage the child to sit on the ride-on toy.

If the child does not take initiative, go ahead and place him back on the ride-on toy.

It is important for the child to develop all gross motor skills required for a ride-on toy.

Continue this daily to help the child get used to a ride-on toy.

Other activities that will assist in developing these skills include climbing a small step stool.

Always monitor the child carefully when he is engaging in gross motor activities; the child can fall easily.

Gross Motor Skills Game

Activity: Crawl Time

Goal: Increase Gross Motor Skills

Supplies:

- ✓ Open space to crawl
- ✓ 3 small pillows
- ✓ Child's toy or doll

Implementation:

Place 3 small pillows strategically around the room.

Place the child's doll or toy on one of the pillows.

Bring the child to the center of the room.

Show the child how the toy or doll moves around the room and over the pillows.

Demonstrate how to crawl over the pillows.

Instruct the child to crawl around the room.

If the child does not want to crawl, place a favorite toy in the room and encourage the child to get the toy.

Encourage the child to crawl over the pillows.

After the child is familiar with crawling around and over the pillows, introduce crawling like a familiar animal.

Begin by talking about a dog; describe crawling around on all four legs like a puppy.

Demonstrate how to crawl around and bark like a puppy.

Afterward, try the same process with a cat.

Crawling is a great cross-lateral exercise.

Gross Motor Skills Game

Activity: Bubble Time

Goal: Increase Gross Motor Skills

Supplies:

- ✓ Open space or outdoors
- ✓ Bubble solution and wand
- ✓ Learning Basket

Implementation:

Bring the child to the center of the room with the Learning Basket.

Tell the child you are going to play with bubbles.

Demonstrate how to create the bubbles.

Tell the child you are going to blow the bubbles, and you both will try to pop the bubbles.

Start with a few bubbles.

Demonstrate how to pop the bubbles by waving your hands and arms up high.

Repeat the process of blowing the bubbles up high along with the waving motion.

Next, blow the bubbles so they are down low.

Demonstrate how to bend down low to pop the bubbles.

Repeat the process of blowing the bubbles down low and bending down low.

Next, blow the bubbles so some of the bubbles remain on a pillow or the floor.

Demonstrate the process of lifting your foot and stomping.

Repeat the process of blowing the bubbles and lifting your feet to pop the bubbles.

Blow the bubbles to the side and slightly away from the child.

Demonstrate how to reach to the side to pop the bubbles.

Repeat the process.

Gross Motor Skills Game

Activity: Hula Hoop

Goal: Increase Gross Motor Skills

Supplies:

- ✓ 3 hula hoops
- ✓ 1 jump rope

Implementation:

Child must be walking well for this activity.

Tell the child you are going to play a game with hula hoops and a jump rope.

Bring the hula hoop out and show the hoop to the child; describe the hoop including its shape and color.

Bring the rope to the center of the room; describe the rope's color and the fact it can make many shapes.

Demonstrate the shapes the rope can make (circle, triangle, square); the child should not know shapes at this age, but this is a great way to continue to teach and introduce items early.

Place the rope out in the room in a straight line.

Demonstrate how to step over the straight line

Allow the child to try independently, and if needed, take the child's hand

Walk with him and assist him to step over the rope.

Continue to practice this skill.

Next, place the hula hoops in a couple of places in the room.

Sit the child in the middle of the hula hoop.

Watch the child crawl out of the hoop.

Describe "in" and "out" by placing the child in and out of the hoop.

Show the child how to step in to the hoop and out of the hoop.

Personal-Social Skills

Activity: Patience

Goal: Personal-Social Skills of Waiting and Delayed Gratification

Supplies:

- ✓ None required

Implementation:

At this age, the child should be able to wait for just a few minutes.

Practice patience with the child as often as possible.

If the child asks for a specific toy, ask him to sit down and wait a moment.

If the child protests, tell him to wait just a moment and you will give him the toy.

If the child continues to protest, do not give him the toy or object he was looking to receive.

Try again later.

Also, try to teach patience when the child is waiting to go somewhere.

Tell the child you are going to the library; go ahead and start a routine of a morning activity: snack, dry diaper and then off to the library (any type of routine is fine).

After the routine has been completed, tell the child you need to grab one more thing; this will assist him with patience in waiting for you (do not leave the child alone but take him with you to get the object required).

Another great time to teach patience is during mealtime.

Make the child wait for just a few minutes to get her food.

Any opportunity to teach patience should be utilized.

Personal-Social Skills

Activity: I Can Help

Goal: Develop Personal-Social Skills

Supplies:

- ✓ Toys and books
- ✓ Toy box, bin or tub
- ✓ Laundry

Implementation:

At this age, the child likes to begin to help.

Provide opportunities for the child to assist you.

A great way to provide these opportunities is with the laundry.

After laundry has been completed by you or the parents, fold everything and tell the child she can help.

Tell the child to get a pair of socks and take them to her room.

Advise the child to place the socks in her correct location.

Next, instruct the child to go back to the laundry.

Hand the child a washcloth; Assist the child with placing the washcloth in the correct place.

Another activity that fosters helping skills is cleaning up toys.

Personal-Social Skills

Activity: Imitate Me

Goal: Develop Personal-Social Skills

Supplies:

- ✓ Two Children

Implementation:

Playing with other children is very important for a child's development.

At this age, the child is engaging in parallel play (the child plays beside or near her playmates but not actually with her playmate).

It is very important for children to interact and play with other children, especially if the children stay at home alone during the day with the caregiver.

Set up play dates or take the child to the park or to story time at the library to encourage interaction with other children.

During the play date, observe how the child interacts with the other children.

You should see that the children are all playing beside each other but not necessarily together.

Next, you will see the children start to imitate each other.

For example, if one child is pretending to play mommy and feed the baby, the other child will start to pretend she is playing mommy and feeding the baby as well.

If one child is playing cars and garage, the other child will want to play cars and garage.

Encourage the children's play by playing with them, as well as providing a nice selection of toys/activities for the children.

If the child is not interacting with a toy, encourage the child by playing with her.

CreativCare Learning Guides

Personal-Social Skills

Activity: Family Time

Goal: Develop Personal-Social Skills and Interaction

Supplies:

- ✓ Mealtime with the family
- ✓ High chair
- ✓ Child plate, cup, utensils
- ✓ Bib

Implementation:

Eating meals as a family or with the child is very important.

If you cannot have a full meal prepared, eat a snack with the child.

It is just as important that the caregiver have lunch with the child as well.

The social interaction this activity provides is invaluable.

Eating with the child enables you to describe the food's color, texture and taste.

Describe each food on the child's plate and try to use fun terms.

For example, if the child is having mashed potatoes, tell her they are sand and the gravy is the lake.

Try to make the food attractive by requesting that the parent purchase some fun items, such a Mickey Mouse cheese.

You can dance the cheese around or play additional games.

Mealtime will continue to be important and will grow in importance as the child becomes older.

Mealtime provides excellent caregiver and family interaction.

Personal-Social Skills

Activity: Drinking from a Cup

Goal: Develop Personal-Social Skills

Supplies:

- ✓ Bib
- ✓ High chair
- ✓ Sippy cup
- ✓ Water

Implementation:

Learning to use a cup is a skill that is needed not only for growing up but also to keep your child's teeth healthy.

If a child continues to use a bottle after 12 months of age, the bacteria from the bottle can gather and provide infection in the teeth and mouth. Using a bottle after 12 months of age can also cause the front teeth to push out, requiring an orthodontist later in life.

Start with ¼ cup or less of water in a Sippy cup.

After meals, give the child ¼ cup of water in the Sippy cup.

Place the cup in front of the child and watch his reaction.

If needed, assist the child with moving the cup to his mouth.

Place the cup back on the high chair table and let the child explore.

Continue with providing the Sippy cup after meals and snacks.

After the child has mastered the Sippy cup, remove the lid from the Sippy cup and add ¼ cup water.

Continue to work with the child in the same way until she has mastered the cup without a lid.

Another great way to teach a young child to drink from a cup is by using plastic cups with Sippy straws.

Personal-Social Skills Game

Activity: Let's Shop

Goal: Increase Personal-Social Skills and Imagination

Supplies:

- ✓ Play food or boxes from food used in the house
- ✓ Shelves or cardboard boxes or fabric boxes
- ✓ Chairs, tables
- ✓ Purse or wallet
- ✓ Pretend money
- ✓ Shopping basket or plastic bucket

Implementation:

Set up the child's playroom or another room using chairs, tables, shelves or cardboard boxes.

Place the different food groups into each box. (Ex: Fruit in one area, meat in another, bread in another, and vegetables in another).

Tell the child you are going to play grocery store.

Tell the child to get his/her purse or wallet.

Use pretend money.

Instruct the child to get the shopping basket.

Talk about the food groups in each section; it is never too early to teach good nutrition.

Ask the child to choose food from each container.

Describe each food chosen, including the color, consistency, type and food group.

Tell the child this is how parents (or you) shop in the grocery store to provide food.

Continue to play store on a regular basis.

Personal-Social Skills Game

Activity: Chores

Goal: Increase Personal-Social Skills and Responsibility

Supplies:

- ✓ Mini play broom and adult broom
- ✓ Cleaning cloth or Swiffer

Implementation:

Tell the child he will be helping with the chores around the house.

It is never too early to start teaching a child about chores and responsibility.

Demonstrate with the large broom how to use a broom.

Place the child's broom out and ask her to sweep like you.

If the child is confused, demonstrate how to use the child's broom.

Tell him that by using the broom, he is doing chores.

Continue working with the broom on a weekly basis.

Next, begin another chore, such as dusting.

Dusting is a perfect chore, but be careful if the child has allergies or asthma.

Take your dusting cloth and begin dusting.

Swiffer is an excellent choice, as no spray is used.

Give the child the Swiffer or cloth and watch him.

If the child needs assistance, show him how to dust.

As the child continues to grow in his development, doing chores will allow him to develop responsibility.

Personal-Social Skills Game

Activity: Sharing and Caring

Goal: Increase Personal-Social Skills and Imagination

Supplies:

- ✓ Dolls or stuffed animals
- ✓ Fisher Price Little People or Weebles

Implementation:

Toddlers become very independent and do not like to share.

One way to promote sharing is by example.

Always try to share with the child if possible.

Work with the child when she has a toy by asking her if you can see the toy for a moment.

Take the toy and then immediately give the toy back.

Practice this frequently.

Another way to teach sharing is by demonstrating sharing with the child's toys.

Set up several dolls and stuffed animals.

Have one doll or toy speak to another toy and ask to share an item.

Continue this process with each stuffed animal.

Read books about sharing to the child.

If allowed, let the child watch one episode of a favorite cartoon about sharing (ex: Dora or Bubble Guppies).

Language Skills

Activity: Name it

Goal: Expressive language skills

Supplies:

- ✓ None Required

Implementation:

Walk around the house with the toddler and name everything you see.

Take the toddler to the kitchen and say "table; see the table where we eat."

"Cup; see the red cup we use to drink milk and water."

"Plate; see the blue plate we use to eat food."

"Picture; see the picture of the baby on the wall."

"Couch, see the tan and green couch where we sit."

Everything you can do to describe at this age is helpful.

When the toddler points to something, describe the object.

When the toddler points to something and wants that object, do not allow her to have the object by simply pointing.

Ask the toddler what item he wants.

Ex: "The cup; do you want the cup?"

If you give the toddler what he is pointing to without describing the object, the toddler has no reason to talk.

By naming objects on a daily basis and describing the objects, the toddler will have a larger vocabulary.

Always encourage the toddler to use his words.

Describe, Describe, Describe!

Language Skills

Activity: Echo

Goal: Expressive language skills

Supplies:

- ✓ None Required

Implementation:

As your child is walking around the house and playing, listen to what she is saying.

When your child says a word, repeat the word.

After repeating the word, describe something else about the word.

If your child says "puppy," repeat the word "puppy" immediately.

Add a statement such as "isn't the puppy cute?" or "what color is the puppy?"

Try to repeat as many words as possible with your child.

Use dressing time as a time to list body parts.

For example: "Foot; let's put your foot into your shoe."

"Hold your hands up high; put your right leg into your pants."

Start with manners by always saying "please" and "thank you."

Make sure your child says "please" when she asks for anything.

Make sure your child says "thank you" when she receives anything.

Language Skills

Activity: Which One

Goal: Receptive language skills

Supplies:

- ✓ Shoe
- ✓ Cup
- ✓ Block
- ✓ Learning Basket

Implementation:

NOTE: Make sure the objects that you have are objects that the child knows and use no more than 3 objects.

Place each object in the Learning Basket.

Ask the child to sit on the floor.

Bring the Learning Basket over to the child.

Take the block out of the basket and ask the child "what is this object?"

After the child says "block," repeat the word "block."

Take the cup out of the basket and ask the child "what is this object?"

After the child says "cup," repeat the word "cup."

Take the shoe out of the basket.

After the child says "shoe," repeat the word "shoe."

Next, place each object back into the Learning Basket.

Take each object back out of the basket without naming the object; place each object on the floor in a line.

Ask the child to give you the cup.

Repeat this process with each item.

The next day, vary the game by placing the objects back in another location in the line (ex: if the block was in the middle, place it on the end). Mix up the objects and repeat the process.

CreativCare Learning Guides

Language Skills

Activity: Sing a Song

Goal: Expressive language skills

Supplies:

- ✓ Words to children's songs
- ✓ Children's song CD
- ✓ CD player

Implementation:

Music is an excellent and fun language tool.

During the day, play children's music in the background.

Make sure to vary the type of children's music (there are rock bands with songs; Fisher Price has songs, church songs, Baby Einstein, etc.).

You may wish to have a specific time of the day to play the children's songs.

It is important to have a music time as part of the child's daily routine.

Make up simple motions to the songs.

Teach the child the motions.

As you sing the songs during the day, you will notice that the child starts to try to sing as well.

Use opportunities during the day to sing the songs the child has been hearing.

Example:

When it is diaper changing time, use this time to sing the songs. This will distract the child from diaper changing, as well as increase vocabulary.

Language Skills

Activity: I Command You

Goal: Receptive Language skills

Supplies:

- ✓ Shoe
- ✓ Book

Implementation:

NOTE: Make sure the objects that you have are objects that the child knows and only use 1 part commands.

Ask the child to join you at the table and have a seat.

Tell the child that today we are going to play a game and see how well you can listen.

Please turn your listening ears on.

Place a book on the floor.

Ask the child to go and get the book.

If the child has difficulty, ask if you may assist.

If the child still has difficulty, take them by the hand and go get the book

Place the child's shoes by the chair ; Ask the child, "Where are your shoes?"

Assist the child as needed.

All of these commands are one-step commands; make sure not to use two-step commands. For example, Go get the book and bring it to me

Language Skills Game

Activity: Game: What Does This Do?

Goal: Receptive language skills

Supplies:

- ✓ Construction paper and glue
- ✓ Picture of a cup
- ✓ Picture of a fork
- ✓ Picture of a coat
- ✓ Picture of a chair
- ✓ Picture of a ball
- ✓ Learning Basket

Implementation:

Cut out pictures and paste them individually on a piece of construction paper.

Place the pictures in the Learning Basket.

Ask the child to join you in the center of the floor.

Tell the child you are going to play a game.

Explain the rules of the game.

Rule 1: Pick a picture out of the Learning Basket.

Rule 2: The caregiver will ask what the item's use is. If the child does not know, give her a hint.

Example:

The child pulls out the cup.

"What do we use this object for?"

The child says "no" or I don't know the answer.

Caregiver response: "When we have breakfast, we use the cup for our milk" (mimic a drinking motion).

If the child still does not know, tell her "we use a cup to drink."

Follow each step above for each object chosen from the Learning Basket.

After all pictures of the items have been removed from the Learning Basket, place the pictures back into the basket; mix up the pictures and start the game again.

CreativCare Learning Guides

Language Skills Game

Activity: ABC's Book

Goal: Expressive language skills

Supplies:

- ✓ Construction paper (different colors with holes already punched) and glue stick
- ✓ Hole punch
- ✓ Ribbon or yarn
- ✓ Pictures of basic words that can be cut
- ✓ Learning Basket
- ✓ Child's small table and chairs

Implementation:

Ask the child to join you at the child's table.

In the Learning Basket, have construction paper (different colors that already have three holes punched along the side).

Show the child some magazines and tell her you are going to start making an ABC book.

Tell her "The first letter of the alphabet is A. What begins with A?" Name several items that begin with A.

Next, find a picture in the magazine that starts with A.

CreativCare Learning Guides

Ask the child to name the picture.

Repeat the name of the picture to the child.

Carefully cut the picture out of the magazine.

Let the child choose a piece of construction paper and make sure to name the color.

Allow the child to use the glue stick to place glue on a construction paper page.

Let the child assist with placing the picture on the page.

Write the name of the picture underneath.

Each day, complete 2-3 letters make a book that has more than one picture for each letter.

Tie the book together using ribbon or string.

Language Skills Game

Activity: ABC's on the Refrigerator or on the Learning Laptop

Goal: Expressive and Receptive Language skills

Supplies:

- ✓ Magnetic ABC Letters; Leap Frog Refrigerator ABC's; Leap Top Learning Laptop
- ✓ See and Say Animals

Implementation:

It is fine to use tools and toys that are already made.

Take the alphabet magnetic letters or use the Leap Top Refrigerator unit to teach letters, phonics and words.

Decide to have a letter of the day.

Take that letter and place the magnetic letters or the refrigerator unit letters in a specific spot on the refrigerator.

Ask the child "what is the letter of the day?"

Tell the child the letter of the day (Example: "B").

Describe the sound that B makes or use the refrigerator unit

CreativCare Learning Guides

Discuss words that begin with B.

Go back to the refrigerator several times a day to remind the child of the letter of the day.

Use the Leap Top Laptop or something similar to learn letters and words; follow the directions given by the computer.

Another fun idea is to help the child use the See and Say with animals and animal sounds.

Make sure to work with the child using these toys, but also give her time to explore the toy alone.

Chapter 4: Eighteen to Twenty-Four Months

Toddlers at this age demonstrate gross motor skills of kicking a ball, fine motor skills of drying hands, language skills of responding to two-part requests and developing a larger vocabulary, and cognitive skills of matching colors.

The top four skills for this age group are:

- ❖ Responding to two-part commands
- ❖ Taking off socks and shoes
- ❖ Speaking at least 20 understandable words
- ❖ Identification of body parts

The top four educational toys for this age group are the following:

- ❖ Building play sets
- ❖ Children's basketball goal and ball
- ❖ 3-6 piece puzzles
- ❖ Shape Sorter

CreativCare Services Milestones (18-24 Months)

	Developmental Category	Developmental Milestones
☐	Language	Speaks 10-20 recognizable words, mixing jargon with intelligible words
☐		Echoes the last word spoken
☐		Names body parts on self, others and in pictures
☐		Names 1 or more pictures
☐		Combines 2 or more words
☐		Responds to a two-part command
☐		Points to 5 or more pictures when named
☐		Uses some prepositions
☐	Motor	Walks up stairs alone
☐		Runs several feet without falling
☐		Squats
☐		Kicks a ball; holds small ball
☐		Strings large beads
☐		Pushes and pulls objects; turns knobs
☐		Scribbles confined to page
☐		Moves to music

NOTE: All children develop at different rates. The above milestones are general guidelines for children's development. Some children are advanced in specific areas and behind in others. Consult your child's Pediatrician if there are questions or concerns.

CreativCare Learning Guides

CreativCare Services Milestones (18-24 Months)

	Developmental Category	Developmental Milestones
☐	Cognitive	Places 6 pegs in a form board
☐		Searches for ways to activate a new toy
☐		Symbolic play
☐		Places 3 shapes in a form board
☐		Finds hidden object under one of two cups
☐		Understands about parts as a whole and belonging to certain groups
☐		Able to make simple decisions when given the choice of two
☐		Plays with several objects and knows when one is missing
☐	Personal-Social	Actively helps dress and undress herself
☐		Looks for and recognizes a friend
☐		Understands "mine"
☐		Generally follows direction related to daily routine
☐		Assists with household chores, putting things away
☐		Shows pride in accomplishments; shows shame
☐		Brushes teeth with training toothpaste
☐		Drinks from a cup with no lid

NOTE: All children develop at different rates. The above milestones are general guidelines for children's development. Some children are advanced in specific areas and behind in others. Consult your child's Pediatrician if there are questions or concerns.

This page is intentionally left blank

CreativCare Learning Guides

CreativCare Montessori Based Learning Guide

Ages: 18-24 Months

Cognitive Skills

Activity: Shapes All Around

Goal: Cognitive Skills and Problem-Solving Skills Enhancement

Supplies:

- ✓ Shape sorter, such as Melissa and Doug, or other complex sorter
- ✓ Form board with shapes
- ✓ Learning Basket
- ✓ Child's small table and chairs

Implementation:

Ask the child to join you at the table and have a seat.

Bring the Learning Basket over with the form board and shape sorter.

Tell the child you are going to talk about shapes.

Pull the shapes from the form board and place them in front of the child.

Ask the child to name the shapes as you point to them one by one.

If the child has difficulty, ask if you may assist and advise the child of the name of each shape.

Ask the child to name the shapes again.

If the child is still having difficulty, move on to another task and come back to the names another time.

Place the form board in front of the child and ask her to match the shapes.

If she has difficulty, ask if you may assist and place the shapes into the form board.

If the child can match the shapes, turn the form board around and see if she is still able to match the shapes.

After the child has mastered naming the shapes and completing the form board, move on to the shape sorter.

Note: Most of the shapes in the shape sorter will be an emerging skill at this age.

Make sure you have the more sophisticated shape sorter with multiple types of shapes rather than a general 3 or 4 shape sorter.

A great example is a shape sorter is the wooden box by *Melissa and Doug*.

Place the sorter in front of the child and tell her this is a type of puzzle.

Tell her, "We are going to work on this puzzle by dumping all the shapes."

Allow the child time to review the shapes and hold them in her hands.

Discuss the color, texture and what the shape is; show the child how to run her fingers along the sides of the shape, counting sides.

Assist the child by showing her how to grab a shape and then see where it fits in the sorter.

Afterward, give the child the same shape and see if she is able to locate the correct space.

CreativCare Learning Guides

Cognitive Skills

Activity: It's All the Same

Goal: Cognitive and Logic Enhancement

Supplies:

- ✓ 3 purple socks
- ✓ Block
- ✓ Shoe box with lid
- ✓ Child's small table and chairs
- ✓ Learning Basket

Implementation:

Place 3 socks of the same color and a block inside a shoe box; place the lid on the box and put it in the Learning Basket.

Ask the child to join you at the table and have a seat.

Tell her you are going to learn about things that are the same and things that are different.

Place the box in front of the child but ask her not to open the box.

Remove each purple sock from the box, saying, "here is a purple sock, here is another purple sock and another purple sock; they are all the same."

Place the socks in a row.

Next, place each of the socks, one by one, back into the Learning Basket, leaving the block in the closed box.

Ask the child to place all the objects that are the same on the table.

If the child has difficulty, ask her to place the socks on the table.

Take the box and look inside; remove the object from the hidden box and name the object for the child; state that the block is different from the socks.

Encourage the child to explore the block.

Ask the child to assist you with placing everything back in the box.

Ask the child to hand you the block; if she hands you a sock, say "thank you for the sock."

Continue this activity and increase the complexity (Ex: use a greater number of objects and objects that are more difficult to distinguish, such as pens, highlighters, pencils, etc.).

Cognitive Skills

Activity: Figure it Out

Goal: Cognitive and Problem-Solving Enhancement

Supplies:

- ✓ Windup toy (or toy with buttons to operate)
- ✓ Toy with a switch
- ✓ Learning Basket
- ✓ Child's small table and chairs

Implementation:

Note: Toys must be something that the child has not played with before.

Place two different toys that have buttons, something to wind, and something with a switch in the Learning Basket.

Ask the child to join you at the table and have a seat.

Tell the child you are going to play with a brand new toy.

Advise the child the name of the toy, such as "it is a xylophone."

Take the toy from the Learning Basket and place it in front of the child.

Allow ample time to explore the toy.

Afterward, ask the child if she can make the toy work.

CreativCare Learning Guides

Tell her the toy should drive across the room or play music; "Can you make it work?"

At this age, the child should take the time to explore the toy and try hard to figure out how to make the toy work.

A younger child will probably get frustrated and leave the toy.

If the child is getting frustrated, ask if you may assist and demonstrate how to turn on the toy.

Give the toy back to the child and let him continue to explore.

If the child is frustrated again, show her how to work another feature of the toy.

Continue this process until the child can fully work the toy.

This may take several sessions with the toy.

During the next week or two, try the other toy.

This type of activity helps the child to focus and develop problem-solving skills.

Cognitive Skills

Activity: My Book for Concentration

Goal: Cognitive Enhancement; Concentration Development

Supplies:

- ✓ Learning Basket
- ✓ Colored construction paper
- ✓ Scissors
- ✓ Hole punch
- ✓ Yarn, three ring binder
- ✓ Pictures of individual objects
- ✓ Child's small table and chairs

Implementation:

Preparation - Obtain pictures of individual objects, such as a pull toy or clothes, dogs etc., and make sure the pictures are only of the objects and nothing else; make sure the pictures are real pictures from magazines, etc. Do not use cartoon pictures.

Example: Picture of a sweater, not a sweater and pants; a picture of a pull toy, not the child pulling the toy; a picture of a dog, not the dog doing an activity, etc.

Create a small book for the child by using colored construction paper and a hole punch; you can use yarn to attach the book or use a three ring binder.

Place the pictures on the right side of the book and leave the left page blank.

Make a picture for the cover so you know what book you are working with at the time.

Ask the child to join you at the table and have a seat.

Have the booklet in the Learning Basket.

Tell the child you are going to look at a book.

Start by talking about the picture on the cover; describe all aspects of the picture.

Next, allow the child to turn the page and then, using your finger, point out every aspect and detail of the picture.

Afterward, let the child explore the book by herself

Talk with the child about how all of the pictures in the book belong to the same family after she has completed the activity. (Example: All of the items in the book are clothes, etc.).

Continue to work with this book on a regular basis.

Add to the pictures of the book as the child gets more comfortable with understanding the current pictures.

An emerging skill would be to introduce pictures with more detail to the book.

Example: Not only should you show the sweater, but also show a picture of a child putting on a sweater; Not only show an apple, but also show someone biting the apple.

All of these activities assist the child in learning about parts as a whole.

Cognitive Skills

Activity: I Decide

Goal: Cognitive and Decision-making Enhancement

Supplies:

- ✓ None Required

Implementation:

At this age, the child is starting to be more assertive and working to gain more independence. It is never too early to teach the child about decision making, while allowing her to assert her independence.

During the child's day, allow her to make simple decisions.

Never give the child more than 2 choices at the time; she is not quite ready for 3 choices.

Meal time is an excellent opportunity to present choices.

Example: "Would you like to wear the puppy bib or the lion bib?" Show the child the objects when giving her choices.

Example: "What would you like for lunch? Mac N Cheese or peanut butter and crackers?"

Activities also provide an opportunity for choices.

Example: "What would you like to sing during music time today? 'Old MacDonald' or 'The Wheels on the Bus'?"

Example: "Would you like to color or paint today?"

Any time during the day that you can offer a choice assists with the development of decision-making skills.

Do not allow the child to waiver; she needs to make a decision and stick to that decision.

Do not ask the child what her choice is if she does not have a choice.

Example: Your lesson plans are all built around a farm today and learning about the animals; the child would not have a choice during music time, so do not offer him a choice.

Example: The parent has said the child will have cheese and crackers for lunch; do not offer the child another option.

There are always going to be decisions to be made in life, so this is the beginning of teaching the child how to make decisions.

Cognitive Skills Game

Activity: Every Day Sounds

Goal: Cognitive and Auditory Enhancement

Supplies:

- ✓ Phone
- ✓ Dishwasher
- ✓ Washing machine
- ✓ Microwave
- ✓ Timer

Implementation:

Part of cognitive development is learning to use all of your senses to solve problems.

Preparation: Record several household sounds, such as the ones that will be made by the supplies listed above.

Note: Start with 3 sounds for the first session.

Ask the child to join you at the table and have a seat.

Tell her you are going to learn all about sounds and how to listen for different sounds; "Make sure your listening ears are turned on."

Play each sound and tell the child after each sound what the object is called.

Play the first sound again and ask the child, "what does that sound like?"

Give her a choice between the phone and dishwasher.

If she is incorrect, ask her to listen again carefully.

Tell the child the sound if she needs assistance.

Continue going through the sounds.

The goal is to develop listening skills and skills of problem-solving.

The child should eventually be able to hear the washing machine and know it is the washing machine.

Practice the sounds daily as they arise during your time together.

Cognitive Skills Game

Activity: Hide and Seek

Goal: Cognitive and Fine Motor Enhancement

Supplies:

- ✓ 5 plastic animals
- ✓ Sandbox outdoors
- ✓ Shovel and pail

Implementation:

Tell the child you will be playing in the sandbox; if the child does not have a sandbox or space for a sandbox, gather a shower curtain liner and place on the floor and use a Tupperware container for the sand indoors.

Show the child the animals in the pail; allow the child to play with and explore the animals.

Tell the child you are going to play a game like hide and seek; the animals will be hidden in the sand and the child will try to find them.

Each time the child finds an animal, she should pick it up with the shovel and place it in the pail.

Demonstrate by hiding the first animal in the child's view and show her how to use the pail and shovel.

Next, ask the child to turn around and do not peek until you call her.

Hide the animals throughout the sand.

Ask the child to turn around.

Tell her it is her turn to find the animals; "remember you are looking for (list the animals that are hidden and their color)."

Let the child explore the sand looking for the animals.

If the child is struggling, ask if you may assist and help her to find one animal.

Repeat the same process as above.

Make sure the toys you are hiding can be washed and are ok to be in the sand.

After the child is more comfortable with the game, ask the child if she would like to hide the animals.

Cognitive Skills Game

Activity: Missing Word

Goal: Cognitive and Expressive Language Enhancement

Supplies:

- ✓ 2 board books that the child likes
- ✓ Rocking chair or couch

Implementation:

Begin this exercise days in advance by reading the same two books over and over; repetition is very important to children.

Place the child in your lap in a rocking chair or beside you on the couch.

Tell him you are going to play a game called missing word.

Let the child choose the book and read it through one more time, being very descriptive regarding the pictures and the content of the book.

Tell him you are going to read the book again, and this time the child will help you.

Start with the title and leave out the last word.

Example: *Dora Goes to the* _____

Run your fingers along the words one by one; when you get to the word that should be "Zoo," leave out the word.

CreativCare Learning Guides

Ask the child, "Dora Goes to the 'What,' what is the missing word?"

If the child does not know, assist him and show him the picture of the zoo on the front of the book.

Continue this process, omitting different words such as the first word or the middle word.

Example: *Dora and _____ are Going to the Zoo*

Ask the child, "Dora and who are going to the zoo? Point to the picture of Boots, while asking the child who is going to the zoo.

This is all a part of early word recognition.

The child will see the picture and associate the correct word, a form of early reading.

Continue to play this game on a weekly basis.

Fine Motor Skills

Activity: Scribble Time

Goal: Fine Motor Enhancement

Supplies:

- ✓ Crayons (regular size)
- ✓ Coloring book or plain white paper
- ✓ Child's small table and chairs
- ✓ Learning Basket

Implementation:

Ask the child to join you at the table and have a seat.

Bring over the Learning Basket with a coloring book, crayons, and a white piece of paper.

Tell the child today we are going to draw a picture or color in the coloring book.

Allow the child to choose the coloring book or paper.

Provide the child with the crayons and ask him to choose only 3 crayons.

Count the crayons as he chooses and selects them.

Give the child time to color and scribble in any way he likes.

Afterward, demonstrate how to color by staying within the lines.

The child will not be able to stay within the lines, but it is good for the child to watch the proper way.

Praise the child and talk about the colors of the crayons, what the picture is and add some descriptive terms or a short story to go with the picture he has drawn.

Give the child the choice again of plain paper or another coloring book page.

Follow the same process.

Try to work on this activity at least 3 times a week if possible.

Fine Motor Skills

Activity: Magnet Attraction

Goal: Fine Motor Enhancement

Supplies:

- ✓ Large magnet
- ✓ 3-6 objects that will be attracted to a magnet
- ✓ Child's small table and chairs
- ✓ Learning Basket

Implementation:

Place the magnet and 3-6 objects that will be attracted to the magnet in the Learning Basket.

Ex: Pen, large paper clip, large marble, key, binder clip

Ask the child to join you at the table and have a seat.

Tell him you will be playing with a magnet and several objects that a magnet likes.

Take all of the objects out and place them in a row.

Take the magnet out and hand it to the child.

Allow the child time to explore the magnet and its properties; describe the shape and how it attracts certain objects.

CreativCare Learning Guides

Ask the child for the magnet.

Show the child how to pick up the first object.

Afterward, give the magnet to the child and ask him to pick up the next object.

If the child struggles, ask if you may assist and show him again.

Discuss the properties of all the objects, including their name, color and shape.

Continue this process using other items that a magnet might attract.

Always consider safety, as this age group likes to place things into the mouth; do not use small objects that the child can swallow.

Fine Motor Skills

Activity: String the Beads

Goal: Fine Motor Enhancement

Supplies:

- ✓ Large beads with different shapes and a string
- ✓ Child's small table and chairs
- ✓ Learning Basket

Implementation:

You can make your own beads by going to a craft store and purchasing different beads with holes in each end or you can go online or to a school supply store and buy the colored beads and strings.

Ask the child to join you at the table and have a seat.

Bring over the Learning Basket containing the beads and string.

Tell the child you will be stringing beads.

Place one bead and the string in front of the child.

Discuss the properties of the bead, including color and shape.

Allow the child to explore the bead and the string.

Next, request the bead from the child.

Demonstrate how to place the bead on the string; show the child that if you lift the string, the bead will fall off.

Take another bead out of the basket and place it in front of the child.

Allow the child to explore the bead.

Tell the child to place the bead on the string.

This may take several sessions of practice; do not allow the child to get frustrated.

Demonstrate again as needed; if the child continues to have difficulty, try again the next day.

After the child is able to string one bead, move on to additional beads.

Fine Motor Skills

Activity: Grasp This

Goal: Fine Motor Enhancement

Supplies:

- ✓ Large beads
- ✓ Small blocks
- ✓ Large binder clips
- ✓ Large jar with lid
- ✓ Child's small table and chairs
- ✓ Learning Basket

Implementation:

Place all items in the Learning Basket.

Ask the child to join you at the table and have a seat.

Take the jar out of the basket and place it in front of the child.

Remove the lid from the jar and, using your thumb and forefinger, pick up each object in the basket one by one and place it in the jar.

Describe each object's properties as you go; shake the jar so the child hears the sounds made by the object.

Afterward, smile at the child and say, "Yay, they are all in the jar."

Take all of the objects out of the jar and place them back into the basket.

Next, place the jar in front of the child and ask him to place the objects into the jar.

If the child does not start the activity, ask him if you may assist.

Demonstrate the activity for the child again.

Then, allow the child to try again.

Do not allow the child to get frustrated; try again another time.

Continue this process and change up the objects (keeping safety in mind because toddlers put things in their mouth) for different sound effects.

Fine Motor Skills

Activity: Fun with Play Dough

Goal: Fine Motor Enhancement

Supplies:

- ✓ Play Dough (bought or homemade)
- ✓ Cookie cutters
- ✓ Child's rolling pin
- ✓ Wax paper
- ✓ Child's small table and chairs
- ✓ Learning Basket

Implementation:

Recipe if you choose homemade Play Dough:

3cups flour
1.5cups salt
6tsp. cream of tartar
3tbsp. oil
3 cups water

> Pour all ingredients into a large pot. Stir constantly over medium heat until a dough ball forms by pulling away from the sides. Knead dough until the texture matches play dough (1-2 minutes). Store in plastic container. Should last for at least 3 months.

CreativCare Learning Guides

Ask the child to join you at the table and have a seat.

Bring the Play Dough and cookie cutters in the Learning Basket.

Talk about the color of the Play Dough and its texture.

Place a piece of wax paper in front of the child.

Allow the child to explore the Play Dough, its texture and all of its properties.

Afterward, show the child how to smooth out the Play Dough; use a child's rolling pin if needed.

Demonstrate how to take one of the cookie cutters and make that shape with the Play Dough.

Next, ask the child to choose a cookie cutter and make their shape with the Play Dough.

Using Play Dough is an excellent fine motor activity; working with the dough helps the small muscles develop.

Fine Motor Skills Game

Activity: Baby Blanket Action

Goal: Fine Motor Enhancement

Supplies:

- ✓ Baby blanket
- ✓ Soft ball such as Nerf, Koosh, etc.
- ✓ Learning Basket

Implementation:

Ask the child to join you in the center of the room.

Have the baby blanket and ball in the Learning Basket.

Tell the child you are going to play a game with the blanket and ball.

Ask the child to hold 2 corners of the blanket; you hold the other 2 corners of the blanket.

Show the child how to shake the blanket to make it wiggle.

Continue this process.

Next, put the blanket down and place a ball in the center of the blanket.

You and the child pick up the blanket at the same time.

Demonstrate how shaking the blanket moves the ball all around.

When the ball falls away from the blanket, ask the child to go and get the ball.

This will provide great fun and the child will love the movement and the excitement of chasing the ball.

Try different activities with the ball on the blanket, such as rolling the ball, hopping the ball, and moving the blanket up and down quickly.

Fine Motor Skills Game

Activity: Thumbkin

Goal: Fine Motor Enhancement

Supplies:

✓ Words to "Where is Thumbkin?"

Implementation:

Ask the child to join you at the center of the room.

Sit on the floor, facing the child.

Tell him you are going to play a singing game with your hands.

The game is called "Where is Thumbkin?" to the tune of "Are you Sleeping?"

Ask the child to watch your hands.

Be very careful when you get to "where is tall man?" Have only two fingers then instead of one.

If you don't know the words, they are listed below:

"Thumbkin"

"Where is Thumbkin? (repeat twice)

Here I am. (repeat twice)

How are you today sir? Very well, I thank you.

Run and hide."

The same lyrics continue with "Where is pointer," "tall man," "ring man" and "pinky."

Begin the game by making a fist with your thumb inside.

When you get to the verse that says "here I am," bring whichever finger out and wiggle.

Next, place the finger back when the song says "run and hide."

The final verse is "Where's the whole family?"

Bring out all fingers and wiggle.

Perform the entire song and then ask the child if she would like to try.

The finger exercises are excellent fine motor enhancers.

Fine Motor Skills Game

Activity: Pretend Amusement Park

Goal: Fine Motor Enhancement

Supplies:

- ✓ None Required

Implementation:

Ask the child to join you in the center of the room.

Tell him you are going to play a game pretending to be a roller coaster car at Disney World.

Tell the child to follow your directions and actions.

Say, "We are at Disney World getting ready to ride Space Mountain." Action: Hold hand straight out and say "VROOM, VROOM"

"Up, Up, Up the mountain we go." Action: Move hand up as if going up a hill.

"Down, Down, Down, the mountain we go." Action: Move hand down as if going down a hill.

"Now we are going around a corner." Action: Move hand around in a circle, swerving back and forth.

"Around the corner is a lake where we see the fish go swish, swish, swish." Action: Move your hand back and forth like the fin of a fish.

"And we see a fish go swish, swish, swish."

"Now we are all done and it was loads of fun." Action: Raise your hands and shout "hurray."

Perform this again and, if needed, break the actions up into smaller segments so the child can follow.

Ex: Today you will learn "up and down" and tomorrow you learn the "up and down and around a corner."

Gross Motor Skills

Activity: Kick the Ball

Goal: Gross Motor Enhancement

Supplies:

- ✓ Kickball
- ✓ Yard or park

Implementation:

Tell the child you will be using outside time to play ball.

Take the ball and child outside.

Allow the child time to explore the ball.

Describe the ball, its shape, color and other properties, such as the ability to bounce.

Show the child how the ball moves and bounces.

Next, tell the child that you are going to work on kicking.

Demonstrate how to move your foot in a kicking motion.

Ask the child to perform the action that you just demonstrated; if needed, perform the kicking motion at the same time.

Demonstrate how to kick the ball.

Ask the child to try to kick the ball.

He may miss the ball completely or only kick a short distance. Do not criticize; smile and say "let's try again."

Demonstrate if needed.

Next, let the child practice kicking the ball to you; stand about 1 foot from the child.

Make sure the yard or playground is safe if the child falls.

Continue practicing when possible.

Gross Motor Skills

Activity: Little Climber

Goal: Gross Motor Enhancement

Supplies:

- ✓ Stairs
- ✓ Child's step stool or play stairs (if needed)

Implementation:

You may use stairs in the child's home. If the child's home does not have a set of stairs, you can use a child's stepstool, play stairs or stairs at a friend's house.

At this age, most children can maneuver stairs on their own.

Start the process with whatever stairs are accessible at the time.

If you are using play stairs or a child's step stool, make sure they are next to a wall.

Safety: After you begin this exercise, the child will start to try to master the stairs on his own. Never leave a child unattended with stairs.

As your child learns to walk well, he will begin to try to climb.

An important gross motor skill is the art of climbing and maneuvering stairs safely.

Start by showing the child a picture or reading a book where a child climbs stairs, talking about stairs and how he tries to go up and down.

Take the child and a doll to a set of stairs.

Allow the doll to go up and down; continue this process.

Afterward, take the child's hand and show him how to step up one stair; say, "we are going up, up, up."

Next, help the child step down; say, "we are going down, down, down."

Continue with the process; as the child gets older, he will learn to master walking up and down stairs.

If there are no outside stairs, take the child to a park or other area.

Practice on different stairs.

After completing the above steps, whether you have already done this activity at 12-18 months or you start with it now, move to the next step.

Teach the child to go up and down the stairs by herself with an adult present.

Preferably, use stairs with a rail. If not available, use the wall as a rail.

Start by asking the child to step up on one step, while holding onto the wall or rail (you are right behind him).

If this is difficult, assist the child and continue to work on this activity another day; we do not want the child to get frustrated.

If the first step is easy, ask the child to hold on and step up again.

You can continue to practice even if there are only two steps.

Practice going "Up, Up, Up" and then "Down, Down, Down" the stairs.

Place pillows around the bottom, just in case the child falls. You should also be right behind the child to catch him in the event of a fall.

Continue this process as often as possible until the child masters going up and down stairs safely by himself.

Note: Never allow the child, no matter how skilled, to go up and down stairs by himself at this age.

Gross Motor Skills

Activity: Look Mommy, I Can Multi-Task

Goal: Gross Motor, Coordination, and Receptive Language

Supplies:

- ✓ Small ball

Implementation:

One of the skills a toddler learns at this age is her first effort of multi-tasking (example: carrying a ball and walking with it at the same time).

Ask the child to join you in the middle of the room on the floor.

Ask the child to pick up the ball and walk with it across the room.

Try this using other commands, such as "pick up the ball and place it in the bucket."

Another way to teach multi-tasking is by asking the child to hold the ball while playing with another toy.

Ask the child to hold the ball and then suggest that she go and get her fire truck or kitchen toy, etc.

Ask the child to keep the ball.

If the child drops the ball, ask him to pick up the ball again; then, suggest she plays with the toy.

Try this process with different objects, keeping in mind that sometimes it is easier to hold a larger object when multi-tasking.

Practicing this skill will not only help with coordination and gross motor skills, but will also serve as practice in following two-part commands.

Gross Motor Skills

Activity: Bubble, Bubble Fun

Goal: Gross Motor Enhancement

Supplies:

- ✓ Bubble wrap (large and small)

Implementation:

Place bubble wrap on the floor in several different areas.

SAFETY: Please make sure that you are with the child at all times, especially around the bubble wrap because toddlers like to place things around their neck and head. Also, make sure you throw the bubble wrap away as soon as you are finished with this game.

Tell the child you are going to play a hopping and jumping game.

If the child is unable to jump or hop, simply show him how to march and stomp.

Demonstrate how to jump, hop, march, and stomp on the bubble wrap to make the loud "pop."

Show your excitement by saying "Pop, Pop, Pop, Pop, Pop; the bubble wrap goes pop, pop, pop."

Ask the child to join you going around the room to pop the bubbles.

CreativCare Learning Guides

Show the child how the small bubble wrap sounds different from the large bubble wrap.

Make up new games, such as pop and sing a song or pop to the tune of a song such as BINGO.

Count as you pop the bubbles.

Say your ABCs as you pop the bubbles.

The child will enjoy this activity, and it will assist with gross motor development and emerging skills of jumping and/or hopping.

Gross Motor Skills

Activity: Balloon Chase

Goal: Gross Motor, Coordination, and Receptive Language Enhancement

Supplies:

- ✓ Several balloons (medium size)
- ✓ Ribbon (ensure ribbon is not long enough to go around the neck)
- ✓ Learning Basket

Implementation:

Ask the child to join you on the floor in the center of the room.

Tell the child you will be playing with balloons.

Describe the properties of the balloons, including colors, texture and the fact that balloons float in the air.

Safety: Always monitor the child during this game and make sure the toddler does not put the balloon in his mouth or try to bite the balloon. Ensure the ribbon tied to the balloons is not long enough to go around the child's neck.

Discuss the activity with the child; the balloons will be released and will float in the air and on the ceiling.

Instruct the child to try to get the red balloon.

Allow the child to try to problem-solve on his own, but if no attempt is made to retrieve the balloon, demonstrate how to reach for the balloon and jump up high.

Allow the child to have success by pulling the balloon back down to the ground and then releasing the balloon.

This activity is great for increasing problem-solving skills, as well as the gross motor skills of batting, reaching and jumping.

Gross Motor Skills Game

Activity: Create a Game

Goal: Gross Motor, Coordination, and Receptive Language

Supplies:

- ✓ Push toy
- ✓ Pull toy
- ✓ Child's small table without the chairs
- ✓ Pillows (2 colors)
- ✓ Cloth napkin

Implementation:

Place different activity stations with each object listed above around the room.

Example:

Ride-on, push toy- Push the car to the green chair.

Pull Toy- Pull the train to the kitchen.

Go under the small table and come out the other side.

Go sit on the blue pillow.

Go to the red pillow and place it in the green chair.

Go get the red napkin and fold it once.

Start the stations by demonstrating what the child is to do at each station, one by one.

Next, demonstrate the first station again and then ask the child to follow your directions.

Show the child how to complete that station's activity.

Go to the next station and follow the same process.

After the child has mastered the tasks, create new tasks for the game.

Gross Motor Skills Game

Activity: Little Artist

Goal: Gross and Fine Motor Enhancement, Artistic Abilities

Supplies:

- ✓ Sponges
- ✓ Paint (different colors)
- ✓ Ribbon - 1 foot long
- ✓ Buckets for paint
- ✓ Child's paint smock
- ✓ Poster board or large white paper

Implementation:

This activity will be very messy, so it is best to complete this outside during nice weather.

Take outside: Different sponges (try to obtain the sponges that are animal shapes, etc.); different colors, sizes and shapes; two wide ribbons; three colors of paint; poster board or large white paper

Tell the child we are going to draw and create using paint.

Talk about the different colors of paint that you will use and have the child identify each color.

Allow the child to exam the sponges and all of their properties before painting begins.

Allow the child to explore the ribbons and all of their properties including texture, color, length, etc.

Tell the child that this is a messy but fun game (make sure the parents approve and you are using washable paint, old clothes and the smock); assist the child in putting on the smock.

Begin the process with the sponges.

Dip the sponges in one of the colors.

Show the child how to make "large art" by moving your arms and hands in a wide motion.

If the parent approves, you can even use the child's feet to make art.

Let the child paint whatever picture she wants.

Use all of the different tools. Place the ribbon into the paint.

Allow the child to sling the ribbon across the canvas you have created.

Gross Motor Skills Game

Activity: Game On

Goal: Gross Motor, Language and Cognitive Enhancement

Supplies:

- ✓ Create a toddler game
- ✓ Poster board
- ✓ Child markers
- ✓ Cube
- ✓ Permanent marker

Implementation:

Use the poster board and make several squares of different shapes and different colors.

Example: Two circles, a pentagon, two squares, two triangles, two rectangles, two stars

Take the cube and draw a different shape on each side.

Let the child color the poster board shapes different colors, making sure to color all of the same shape the same color (example: circles will all be red).

Tell the child you are creating a game to play.

Make up the rules to the game anyway you would like.

An idea is the following:

Roll the cube and for each shape where the cube lands, an activity is given to the child.

You should play the game too so the child understands that in most games, we take turns.

Example: The cube is rolled and a blue pentagon is facing upward.

Ask the child to find the blue pentagon on the board. Tell him a pentagon has five sides and assist him if he has difficulty. After he tries to find the blue pentagon, ask him to bring the card to you.

Continue the game until all of the shapes are captured.

Add rules, such as when you draw the circle, crawl over the circle.

Add different motor movements.

Language Skills

Activity: Language Expansion

Goal: Expressive Language Enhancement

Supplies:

- ✓ None Required

Implementation:

At this age, your child should be starting to put two words together. One mistake that many parents make (and it is very easy to do) is to talk the way the toddler talks. It is so cute and you hate to correct the child, but it is very important to use correct grammar and complete sentences when speaking to a toddler.

When your child says two words, such as "I do," expand on what she is trying to say even if you know what she means.

State "What are you doing? Are you playing with blocks?"

Next, expand even more by saying "Are you having fun? Are you building a house?"

It is very important to expand your child's language world.

Other examples are:

Play car - You would say "You are playing with the car. What color is the car? Does the car go 'vroom vroom'?"

Go in- You would say "Would you like to go into the room? What would you like to play in the playroom?"

Take every opportunity you can during the day to talk about things and describe what the toddler is seeing and doing.

This also includes mealtime: "You are eating yellow Mac N Cheese, red grapes and a yellow cracker."

Continue this process and you will see your child's language grow.

Language Skills

Activity: Reading Time

Goal: Expressive and Receptive Language Enhancement

Supplies:

- ✓ Short and simple board books
- ✓ Rocking chair or child's table and chairs
- ✓ Learning Basket

Implementation:

Reading is an essential part of language development. You should read to the toddler at least 10 minutes each day.

This is a good time to start using a small table and chair, which is an essential portion of Montessori teaching.

Place the toddler in the chair.

Bring over the Learning Basket with two board books.

Allow the toddler to choose which book she would like to read.

Begin looking at the books by telling the toddler about the pictures instead of reading the words.

Point to each picture when you discuss the pictures with the child.

Ex: "See the puppy; the puppy is playing ball."

Ask the toddler to point to the puppy or find the puppy.

Ask the toddler, "What is the puppy doing?"

Use sounds during these sessions as well, such as "Woof, woof. Do you hear the puppy barking?"

Toddlers will begin to repeat what you say, so be mindful of using inappropriate words around a toddler.

If the toddler learns an inappropriate word, just ignore the word and the toddler will eventually stop using the word.

Language Skills

Activity: That is a Shoe

Goal: Expressive and Receptive Language Enhancement

Supplies:

- ✓ Doll or stuffed animal
- ✓ Child's small table and chairs
- ✓ Learning Basket

Implementation:

Ask the toddler to join you at the table and have a seat.

Bring the Learning Basket and introduce the doll or stuffed animal to the toddler.

Allow the toddler time to explore the animal or doll.

Afterward, ask the toddler to make the doll stand.

Ask the toddler to point to the animal's or doll's eyes.

If the toddler does not point to the right location, ask him to show you her eyes.

If he is still having difficulty, say "let me help you."

Point to the doll's or animal's eyes and your own eyes.

Next, ask the toddler to point to the doll's shoe or foot.

CreativCare Learning Guides

Follow the same process as noted above.

Finally, ask the toddler to point to the doll's or animal's hair.

Again, follow the same process, only assisting as needed.

A toddler at this age will probably only be able to point to approximately 3 items.

Continue this process each day with the same 3 items until they are mastered.

Afterward, move forward with 3 new items on the doll, animal or the toddler, following the same process.

Language Skills

Activity: Fun with Phonics

Goal: Expressive and Receptive Language Enhancement

Supplies:

- ✓ Picture book with 4-6 pictures starting with the letter C
- ✓ Different colors of construction paper; child safe glue; scissors; pictures starting with the letter C
- ✓ Toddler's small table and chairs
- ✓ Learning Basket

Implementation:

Create a picture book with 4-6 pictures, 1 per page, all starting with the letter C.

Ask the toddler to join you at the table and have a seat.

Bring the Learning Basket containing the picture book.

Tell the toddler you are working with the letter C. Sound out the sounds for letter C phonetically.

Ask the toddler to repeat the sounds.

Show the toddler the first picture in the book.

Ask the toddler "what is this a picture of that begins with C?"

If the toddler does not say, sound out the syllables of the picture.

Example: Car - "Cah ah ah ah R" and then say "car; this is a picture of a blue car. Can you say car?"

If the toddler says the syllables correctly, smile and move on to the next picture; if the toddler does not say the syllable correctly, do not correct him, simply say the correct sounds again.

Ask the toddler to try to say "Cah, ah ah ah R, CAR." If he still has difficulty, move on to the next picture.

Do not allow him to get frustrated; tell him we will talk more about C words another day.

If the toddler is doing well, continue with the pictures following the same process.

The next day, come back to the book; see if the toddler can name the pictures and if he can move on to the next phase.

Ask the toddler to name other things that start with a C.

Assist him as needed by naming other C items such as cat, cookie, coat, card, cup, etc.

Language Skills

Activity: Follow Directions

Goal: Expressive and Receptive Language Enhancement

Supplies:

- ✓ None Required

Implementation:

During the day, practice directions and commands with the toddler. Make sure the directions are one-step at first.

Example: Go get the ball; Sit down; Where is your shoe?

All of the above are one-step commands.

When a toy is on the floor, ask the toddler to please pick it up.

See if the toddler will follow the direction. If the toddler stands there and acts confused, request again "Please get the car."

If the toddler still stands there, take his hand and go over to pick up the car together.

Try another command and go through the same process.

Make sure to only use the one-step command.

If the toddler can follow all of the one-step commands that you ask, move on to two-step commands.

Example: Go get the ball and bring it to me; Get the car and put it in the bucket.

The same process will be followed for the two-step command.

This process enhances Receptive Language on a daily basis.

Use commands and direction during all daily activities.

Additional examples are:

One-Step:

Come to the table; Bring me the shoe; Where is your coat?; Go get your cup.

Two-Step:

Go get your cup from the table; Come to the table and sit down; Bring me the shoe and place it on the chair; Where are your coat and your hat?; Go get the ball and bring it to me.

Language Skills Game

Activity: It is a Match

Goal: Expressive and Receptive Language Enhancement

Supplies:

- ✓ 3 objects (stuffed animal, apple, pen, etc.)
- ✓ Pictures of the three objects listed above
- ✓ Toddler's small table and chairs
- ✓ Learning Basket

Implementation:

Create picture cards of the objects; you can use magazines, coloring books or draw the pictures yourself.

Ask the toddler to join you at the table and have a seat.

Bring the Learning Basket, which will contain 3 objects with 3 picture cards.

Bring the objects out one at a time.

Example: "Apple; this is a red apple that we eat. Can you say apple?; sound out the syllables of "apple."

If the toddler repeats the word, move on to the next object; if not, try to sound out the word again and have the toddler repeat.

CreativCare Learning Guides

Bring out the next object and place it beside the apple; repeat the same process listed above.

Bring out the third object and place it beside the 2nd object; repeat the same process listed above.

After all objects are in a row, pick them up one by one and repeat the words one more time, as well as asking the toddler to repeat the word.

Afterward, pull out the first picture card and ask the toddler to place the card under the correct object.

If the toddler is struggling, ask if you may assist.

Continue this process until all picture cards are matched.

Point to one of the picture cards and objects and ask the toddler to name the object/picture.

Continue until the child knows the objects.

Next, add three new objects and, as the toddler is more comfortable, add more than 3 objects and pictures.

CreativCare Learning Guides

Language Skills Game

Activity: Hiding Puppy

Goal: Expressive and Receptive Language Enhancement

Supplies:

- ✓ Stuffed puppy
- ✓ Box
- ✓ Child's small table and chairs
- ✓ Child play mat or blanket

Implementation:

Bring the stuffed puppy and the toddler to the play mat or specific space on the floor.

Tell the toddler you are playing a game with the puppy.

Give the puppy to the toddler and tell him to listen to the directions.

Example: "Place the puppy on the floor"; if the toddler follows the command, move to the next command.

"Place the puppy in the box."

"Take the puppy out of the box."

"Place the puppy under the table."

"Place the puppy on the table."

"Place the puppy above your head."

"Place the puppy below your arms."

Continue with the commands.

If at any time the toddler has difficulty with the command, simply go back and assist him with the proper command.

Afterward, ask him to complete the command again.

Continue working with the commands until the toddler is comfortable.

To make the game more interesting, you can add music to the commands such as "I've Been Working on the Railroad," etc.

Language Skills Game

Activity: All About My Day

Goal: Expressive and Receptive Language Enhancement; Early Reading

Supplies:

- ✓ Camera
- ✓ Learning Basket
- ✓ Printer with paper
- ✓ Construction paper
- ✓ Child safe glue or tape
- ✓ Notecard ring or three ring binder
- ✓ Hole punch
- ✓ 5-10 pictures of daily activities
- ✓ Child's small table and chairs

Implementation:

Take pictures of the toddler during his day.

Examples: Playing with blocks, eating lunch, getting ready for a nap, reading time, music time, outside time, getting dressed, playing with a toy

Take the pictures and paste or tape them onto colored construction paper.

Punch holes and place them on a notecard ring or three ring binder.

CreativCare Learning Guides

Make sure to place the pictures in the order they occurred.

Ask the child to have a seat at the table.

Take the picture book out of the Learning Basket.

Let the toddler explore the picture book.

The toddler will be excited to see his pictures.

Show the toddler the first picture and ask him what he sees.

Give the toddler a chance to describe the picture.

Afterward, describe the picture for the toddler.

Example: "You are playing with blocks, stacking the red and blue blocks. You are smiling, and it is playtime."

Go through each picture following the same process.

After the toddler can describe the pictures, start to teach the toddler about sequence of events.

Sequence of events would be an emerging skill at this age, but if the toddler already has a good grasp on the pictures and their descriptions, move forward with teaching him which picture comes first.

Example: Picture of Breakfast, picture of getting ready for nap, picture of story time

CreativCare Learning Guides

Personal-Social Skills

Activity: Brush Your Teeth

Goal: Self-Help Skills Enhancement

Supplies:

- ✓ Toothbrush
- ✓ Training toothpaste (Do not use regular toothpaste until the child is older and understands not to swallow the toothpaste.)
- ✓ Cup with water
- ✓ Children's book about brushing teeth
- ✓ Stuffed animal with teeth
- ✓ Practice toothbrush

Implementation:

Read the toddler a children's book about brushing your teeth.

Talk to the toddler about the importance of brushing her teeth.

Bring a stuffed toy with teeth and the practice toothbrush to the toddler.

Ask the toddler to brush the animal's teeth.

Afterward, demonstrate the proper way to brush teeth.

Use a teeth brushing song such as:

"Brush your teeth; Everyday; Circles small; Gums and all; A small soft toothbrush the round and round way, will keep your gums healthy and

stop tooth decay; So clean very carefully three times a day; Go round and round, round and round."

You can also make up your own song.

Let the toddler brush his own teeth and you brush behind him.

One of the most important times to brush is before bedtime.

Work on teaching the toddler to spit the toothpaste out of her mouth.

To make the activity more interesting use a themed toothbrush, such as Dora or Thomas the Train.

It is recommended that a child see the dentist no later than 2 years of age. Some pediatricians recommend beginning to take the child as early as 1 year.

Personal-Social Skills

Activity: Wash Your Hands

Goal: Self-Help Skills Enhancement

Supplies:

- ✓ Bathroom sink
- ✓ Sturdy step stool
- ✓ Hand soap or themed hand soap (Elmo, etc.)
- ✓ Hand towel or paper towel
- ✓ Coloring book with hand washing pictures
- ✓ Glitter
- ✓ Child's small table and chairs
- ✓ Crayons

Implementation:

Before every meal or snack and after each trip to the potty, make sure the child washes his hands.

Ask the child to join you at the table; bring the Learning Basket with hand washing pictures to color.

Tell the child you are going to talk about making sure your hands are clean.

Tell the child that germs are everywhere and washing your hands is very important.

Allow him to color a picture of hand washing and discuss the picture.

Demonstrate for the child how to wash your hands properly.

- ✓ Warm water
- ✓ Soap
- ✓ Paper towel or hand towel
- ✓ Place some soap into your hands; rub your hands together including between the fingers, the backs of the hands and up the wrists.
- ✓ Place your hands under the water for at least 20 seconds; A child will not know 20 seconds, so hands under water through singing the entire alphabet song, scrubbing vigorously.
- ✓ Dry hands thoroughly with the towel.

Listed below is a more advanced activity for 2 years and above:

To show the child how germs stay on your hands, wet the hands slightly and place glitter on your hands.

Shake the child's hand, showing him the glitter goes from one person to the next.

Next, wash your hands in cold water; some of the glitter remains.

Wash your hands in warm water with no soap; some of the glitter remains.

Follow the steps above with soap and the glitter should be gone.

Discuss this activity, telling the child how germs go from person to person.

CreativCare Learning Guides

Personal-Social Skills

Activity: Take it Off

Goal: Self-Help Skills Enhancement

Supplies:

- ✓ Dress up doll with clothes (Ex: Mickey Mouse)

Implementation:

A child at this age will not necessarily be able to put on his clothes, but he is beginning to take off his clothes.

Bring the child to the center of the room or playroom.

Show him the dress up doll.

Tell him that the doll will teach him how to take off clothes and put on clothes.

Hand the doll to the child and let him explore the doll.

In a few minutes, ask the child to take off the doll's shirt or coat (make sure the coat or shirt is open for the child, without being buttoned or zipped).

If the child does not understand or attempt this task, ask if you may assist and show the child how to take off the doll's coat.

Ask the child to take the coat off again; if the child still has difficulty, move on to another easier task, such as taking the shoe off.

Do not allow the child to be frustrated; if this happens, try the activity the next day.

If the child can take off the coat, ask him to take another article of clothing from the doll.

Continue this process, each time describing what the child is doing.

Discuss how taking the clothes from the doll relates to the child taking off her clothes.

If the child needs changing, allow him to take off his socks (or something simple in the beginning).

To practice this skill, ask the parents if you may change the child once during the day, so the child can practice taking off his clothes.

Request that the parents practice this skill at bedtime as well.

Personal-Social Skills

Activity: Play Date

Goal: Personal-Social Skills Enhancement

Supplies:

- ✓ Play time with other children

Implementation:

Interaction with other children is very important in a toddler's life. It is important to provide play dates or put the child in situations (example: story-time at Barnes and Noble) where there is interaction with other children.

Schedule a play date or take the child to an activity.

When a friend walks in, the child should recognize that the child is familiar and is a friend.

Allow the children to play together in whatever way they choose.

At this age, the children should be playing together and not just side by side (Parallel Play).

If the children are not interacting with each other, go over to the child and interact with him and try to get the play date child to interact.

Example: If your child is playing house and the friend is playing doctor, go over to your child and say, "May I play?"

Engage the play date child to come over and interact with you playing house.

There should be a copying of actions. For instance, if one child is cooking soup, the other child is likely to want to cook soup as well.

This is also an excellent opportunity to work on sharing.

Children this age are usually in a "mine" phase, and it is imperative that they learn to share.

If you see the child is not sharing, tell him, "We need to share our toys."

All of the above skills can be practiced at home with you acting as the play date character.

Personal-Social Skills

Activity: No Spills

Goal: Self-Help Skills Enhancement

Supplies:

- ✓ Child's cup - 2 (toss away cups without lids will work)
- ✓ Drink of your choice (good to start with water)
- ✓ Child's small table and chairs
- ✓ Learning Basket

Implementation:

Earlier, you practiced the art of drinking from a cup. Now, it is time to remove the lid and start another phase.

Ask the child to join you at the table and have a seat.

In the Learning Basket, have a Sippy cup with a lid and some water in the cup; have another cup without the lid containing no liquid.

Tell the child, "Now you are a big girl/boy, and we are going to start drinking from a cup just like mommy/daddy."

Take the cup without the lid or drink and place it in front of the child.

Ask the child to pick up the cup.

If the child tries to use one hand, ask him to please use two hands.

If the cup drops, say, "that is ok; let's try again."

The next step is to show the child how to sip from the cup.

Ask the child to bring the cup to his mouth and pretend to sip.

Next, take the Sippy cup with liquid and remove the lid.

Place the cup in front of the child.

Tell the child, "No lid and we have water."

Ask the child to slowly pick up the cup and sip water.

The child will probably spill the water at first and that is ok; it will take a bit of practice to master this task.

Ask the parents to participate by only giving the child a cup without a lid for meals.

Personal-Social Skills Game

Activity: The Lunch Guest

Goal: Personal-Social and Interaction Skills Enhancement

Supplies:

- ✓ Child's small table and chairs
- ✓ Lunch place setting (plastic plate, plastic cup, utensils, napkin)

Implementation:

Tell the child you will be having a guest visit for lunch.

Say, "Let's set the table for lunch."

Allow the child to carry the plates to the table.

Show the child where to place the plates.

Allow the child to carry the cups to the table.

Show the child where to place the cups.

Repeat the same process with utensils and napkins.

After both places are set, discuss what has been placed on the table; describe the plates, cups and napkins including shapes, colors and purpose of each item.

Example: "We put our food on the plate when we eat."

Next, tell the child she may choose who she would like to invite to lunch.

Make sure the child has a choice between dolls and animals that can sit in a chair.

After the animal is chosen, ask the child to ask the animal or doll if they would like to join you for lunch.

Place the chosen animal or doll in the chair.

Ask the child to sit beside the animal.

Let the child interact with the animal.

If the child does not interact, assist the child by talking with the animal and requesting that the child talk with the animal about lunch.

Example: "Kitty, would you like peanut butter for lunch today? We love peanut butter and it is fun to eat."

Do everything you can to assist with the interaction between the animal and the child.

This will assist with the child's socialization skills.

CreativCare Learning Guides

Personal-Social Skills Game

Activity: Picture This

Goal: Personal-Social and Emotional Skills Enhancement

Supplies:

- ✓ 4 Pictures of your child and 6 pictures of other children
- ✓ Colored construction paper
- ✓ Hole punch
- ✓ Colored yarn
- ✓ Laminate pictures are an option
- ✓ Pretty box is an option
- ✓ Child's small table and chairs
- ✓ Learning Basket

Implementation:

There are two ways to play this game: Option One - glue the pictures on a piece of colored construction paper and make a book, or Option Two - laminate the pictures and place them in a pretty box.

Ask the child to join you at the table and have a seat.

In the Learning Basket, you will have either the booklet of pictures or the box.

If you made the booklet, make sure the 4 pictures of the child are dispersed throughout the book.

Tell the child you will play a game called "who is that toddler?"

Ask the child to either turn to page 1 of the book or pull out a laminated card.

Notice if the child immediately responds, "that is me."

If not and the picture is of the child, ask him to look again. Say, "who is that toddler?"

Ask the child to describe what the child is doing in the picture and different aspects of the picture.

The child should recognize himself in these pictures.

Examples of descriptions for pictures: The little girl has brown hair and blue eyes, and she is playing with a puppy and smiling.

Continue this process of going through the pictures.

Another fun activity is showing the child himself in the mirror; the child should recognize who is in the mirror and even try to make faces.

Personal-Social Skills Game

Activity: Manner Time

Goal: Personal-Social and Emotional Skills Enhancement

Supplies:

- ✓ Child's small table and chairs
- ✓ Child's stuffed animals or doll or Fisher Price Little People
- ✓ Learning Basket

Implementation:

It is never too early to start working on manners with children. The first words related to manners that this age group should learn are "please" and "thank you." Also, teach the child to be respectful of adults.

Set a good example and always say "please" and "thank you" to the child.

When you give him a snack, lunch or toy, request that the child say "thank you."

When the child requests something from you, ask him to say "please."

Another fun way to work on manners is through pretend play.

This could be done using the child's stuffed animals or dolls, but it could also be done by using the Little People series (House; Princess Castle; Airport, etc.).

Demonstrate to the child how the Little People should be using their manners.

If one of the Little People would like to go to the park, have him ask nicely and say "please."

Continue to use pretend play to reinforce manners.

The child is watching you and will imitate the words you are using.

This is an excellent way to enhance social skills.

There are also books and coloring books on manners.

Discuss and practice manners on a daily basis.

Chapter 5: Two to Three Years

Toddlers at this age demonstrate independence and may have tantrums when things do not go their way. The toddler's favorite words are "no" and "mine." A two-year-old should be using utensils to eat and should be drinking from a cup without spilling most of the time.

The top four skills for this age group are the following:

- ❖ Identifies objects by use
- ❖ Uses personal pronouns; knows first name
- ❖ Runs without falling
- ❖ Imagination in play

The top four educational toys for this age group are the following:

- ❖ Play kitchen
- ❖ Child's learning laptop
- ❖ Coloring books
- ❖ Books

CreativCare Services Milestones (2-3 Years)

	Developmental Category	Developmental Milestones
☐	Language	Gives first name upon request
☐		Uses personal pronouns
☐		Recites portions of nursery rhymes or songs
☐		Makes four word utterances
☐		Identifies boy and girl dolls
☐		Understands "one"
☐		Knows names of one of more friends/relatives
☐		Knows prepositions (in, out, on, in front of, toward and behind)
☐	Motor	Opens doors
☐		Jumps forward with both feet
☐		Builds a tower with 6 blocks
☐		Imitates a vertical line
☐		Turns pages of book one at a time
☐		Descends ladder
☐		Holds crayon with thumb and fingers
☐		Draws a circle

NOTE: All children develop at different rates. The above milestones are general guidelines for children's development. Some children are advanced in specific areas and behind in others. Consult your child's Pediatrician if there are questions or concerns.

CreativCare Learning Guides

CreativCare Services Milestones (2-3 Years)

	Developmental Category	Developmental Milestones
☐	Cognitive	Demonstrates auditory memory for 1 picture
☐		Removes lid from a box or jars
☐		Sorts toys for play
☐		Imitates higher level activities, such as housekeeping
☐		Stacks rings on peg according to size
☐		Repeats a two-digit sequence
☐		Understands order and sequence of events
☐		Places 3 shapes in a rotated form board
☐	Personal-Social	Possessive about toys until age 3
☐		Throws tantrums when frustrated
☐		Listens to stories read from a book
☐		Offers object without wanting it back
☐		Indicates toileting needs
☐		Says "no" to adult requests
☐		Is assertive - resists or persists
☐		Participates in simple group activities

NOTE: All children develop at different rates. The above milestones are general guidelines for children's development. Some children are advanced in specific areas and behind in others. Consult your child's Pediatrician if there are questions or concerns.

CreativCare Learning Guides

CreativCare Montessori Based Learning Guide

Ages: 2-3

Cognitive Skills

Activity: Matching Squares

Goal: Cognitive Development

Supplies:

- ✓ 18 cloth squares, 2 of each type (different patterns, colors, textures) approximately same size
- ✓ 1 large piece of colored construction paper
- ✓ Child's glue
- ✓ Basket for supplies
- ✓ Child's table and chairs

Implementation:

Place all materials in the work tray and take to the child's table.

Ask the child to assist you in making some artwork.

Ask the child to pick out a piece of cloth; describe the color, pattern and texture of the chosen square.

Help the child to apply the glue to each corner of the square and in the middle.

Ask the child to place the square in the corner of the piece of construction paper, glue side down.

Continue letting the child choose another square until all 9 types are glued on the page.

Afterward, remove all materials except the page with the squares and the additional 9 matching squares.

Ask the child to choose another square from the extra squares.

Instruct the child to place the square on top of the identical square on the paper.

Repeat the process until all squares are matched.

Each time, describe the squares' color, pattern and texture.

CreativCare Learning Guides

Cognitive Skills

Activity: Puzzle time

Goal: Cognitive Development

Supplies:

- ✓ 4-6 piece puzzles (at least 3)
- ✓ Basket

Implementation:

Place the basket on the floor with 3 completed puzzles inside.

Ask the child to choose 1 puzzle to work first.

Place the 2 puzzles not chosen aside.

Sit on the floor with the child and describe what is on the puzzle (Example: "What do you see on the puzzle? Lions, bears, and monkeys."

Tell the child you will be working on putting the puzzle together.

Take the puzzle and turn it over, dumping all the pieces out.

Let the child assist you in turning all of the puzzle pieces over again.

Explain to the child that you look at the shape and color of the puzzle to figure out where each piece should fit.

Let the child try to fit the first piece of the puzzle .

If the piece fits, praise the child; if the piece does not fit, encourage the child to try again.

If the child is frustrated, advise him that it is ok if it doesn't fit the first time; try again.

Another strategy would be to let the child try another piece of the puzzle.

If the puzzle chosen is too difficult this time, obtain another puzzle that is simpler.

After the child masters this puzzle, have him complete the puzzle 2 more times.

Afterward, let the child choose another puzzle.

Cognitive Skills

Activity: Sequence

Goal: Cognitive ability to sort

Supplies:

- ✓ Basket
- ✓ 10 cardboard squares with pictures (5 Describing activities from morning to night in the life of a 2 year old; 5 describing morning to night in a dog's life)
- ✓ Poster board

Implementation:

Place the poster board in the middle of the floor.

Ask the child to help you gather the basket for today's activity.

In the basket will be the squares that you have prepared.

Tell the child to come and sit with you on floor.

Let the child choose 1 picture from the basket to place on the poster board.

Discuss what is occurring in the picture.

Repeat this procedure with each card that has a picture of the day until all pictures are out of the basket and have been described.

Ask the child to place the pictures on poster board in a row.

As each picture is chosen and placed on the poster board, describe to the child what is occurring in the picture.

When all pictures are on the poster board, ask the child which one comes first.

Point to each picture in the row; when you reach the picture that comes first, place that picture on the other side of the poster board.

Continue until all pictures are in the correct order.

Next, place the pictures back into the basket and see if the child can pick which picture comes first.

An example child sequence would be:

1. Getting out of bed
2. Having breakfast
3. Brushing teeth
4. Bath time
5. Bed

An example dog sequence would be:

1. Breakfast
2. Morning walk
3. Afternoon playtime
4. Bath
5. Bedtime

CreativCare Learning Guides

Cognitive Skills

Activity: Shapes

Goal: Cognitive ability to identify shapes

Supplies:

- ✓ Form board with 3-4 shapes
- ✓ Learning Basket

Implementation

Place the following items in the Learning Basket: Form board with 3-4 shapes

With the child sitting on the floor in the middle of the room, join and describe what is in the Learning Basket.

Pull out each shape and describe the shape, as well as its color.

Line up each shape on the floor and ask the child to pick out the circle.

Repeat process with each shape.

After the child identifies each shape, ask him to place one shape at a time in the form board.

If the child has difficulty, ask if you can assist and show the child where each shape should be placed.

Afterward, place the shapes in a row on one side and the form board on the other side.

CreativCare Learning Guides

Ask the child to place the shapes one at a time.

Allow the child time to work on this activity alone.

If the child seems frustrated, intervene and ask the child if you may help.

Take all shapes out and rotate the form board.

Ask the child to name each type of shape and its color as he tries to figure out where each shape goes.

Continue to review this process.

Cognitive Skills

Activity: Memory

Goal: Cognitive ability to remember one object

Supplies:

- ✓ Alphabet cards (3 different cards)
- ✓ Learning Basket
- ✓ Child's small table and chairs

Implementation

Have the child sit at the table with the Learning Basket.

Place the alphabet cards inside the Learning Basket.

Tell the child you are going to play a game to see what she can recall.

Pull the first alphabet card out of the Learning Basket.

Ask the child what picture is on the card; what letter is on the card.

After the child responds, turn over the first card.

Pull another card from the Learning Basket and repeat the procedure.

Continue this process until all three cards are out of the Learning Basket.

Make sure all cards are out of the Learning Basket and turned over on the table.

Afterward, turn the cards face up again and go over each card name.

Next, show the child each alphabet card and turn them face down.

Ask the child to find one of the cards, touch each card. Ex. monkey

Request that the child find the monkey by asking her to touch the card that is the monkey.

At this particular age, only try this with one memory card.

Continue to repeat the procedure until the child identifies the card requested.

Reverse the procedure and let the child ask you to identify where the monkey is located.

Afterward, repeat the procedure using the two additional cards.

Make sure to have the child looking for only one card at a time.

Cognitive Skills Game

Activity: Making puzzles

Goal: Cognitive Development and Imagination

Supplies:

- ✓ Colored markers or crayons
- ✓ Foam plates
- ✓ Coloring book
- ✓ Safety scissors
- ✓ Laminating machine or use UPS Store
- ✓ Work tray
- ✓ Child's table and chairs

Implementation:

Place all materials in the work tray and take the materials to the child's table.

Explain to the child that you will be making puzzles.

Demonstrate the following activities first:

Take the foam plates and draw different shapes or lines on the plates.

Color each of the sections drawn with markers or crayons.

Cut each section with the safety scissors.

After each section is cut, place the pieces back together.

Another option is to cut shapes out of the foam plate, color the shapes, and then fit the correct shape in the correct place.

Now, show the child all of the materials and step away, allowing him to work on his own.

If the child seems to struggle, ask if you may assist.

Let the child complete the first puzzle and then repeat with at least 3 other foam plates.

Another option that will enable you to actually preserve the puzzles is the following:

Have the child color 3-4 pictures in a coloring book.

Cut out different portions of the pictures.

Take the cut-outs to the UPS store for lamination.

The child can use these homemade puzzle pieces to work on again and again.

Cognitive Skills Game

Activity: Find the Block

Goal: Cognitive Memory Development and Imagination

Supplies:

- ✓ 3 Solo cups or other cups of different colors
- ✓ Blocks
- ✓ Learning Basket

Implementation:

Fill the Learning Basket with supplies.

Ask the child to meet you in the middle of the floor.

Bring the Learning Basket over to the floor.

Tell the child you are going to play a hide and seek game with the block.

Line up the cups.

Ask the child to place the block under one of the cups.

Tell the child to move the cups around, and you demonstrate how to find the block.

Tell the child you have to remember to watch which cup the block is under.

Let the child place the block again and move the cups around.

You will be the one to find the block.

Next, tell the child it is his turn to play the game.

You will place the block under a cup and move the cups.

Ask the child to find the block.

If he does not guess the correct cup, allow him to guess again.

If the child still does not guess the correct cup, start the entire process of placing the block and moving the cups again.

Continue to practice and use other objects under the cups.

Make sure to name the colors and sizes of the objects that you are working with at the time.

Cognitive Skills Game

Activity: Organize My Toys

Goal: Cognitive Development and Sorting

Supplies:

- ✓ Toy cars, Fisher Price Little People, toy house, race track, kitchen set, pots
- ✓ Note: You can substitute all toys with whatever you have available, but you must have 3 categories of toys.
- ✓ 3 boxes

Implementation:

Take the 3 boxes and some of each toy to each box Ex: Each box should contain cars, Little People and pots.

Have the race track, toy kitchen and toy house set up in another location of the room or in another room.

Take all of the boxes and ask the child to join you on the floor.

Tell the child that each box contains cars, Little People and pots.

Show the child how to sort by dumping one box and placing the cars in one place, the Little People in another place, and pots in another place.

Have the child attempt to sort the next box; if she is unable to complete the task, ask if you may assist.

Repeat the same procedure with the final box.

After each box is sorted, let the child help you place the cars into one box, the pots into another, and the Little People into the last box.

Ask the child to tell you which toy the Little People belong with, which toy the pots belong with, and which toy the cars belong with.

Have the child take the cars to the correct toy; repeat with the pots and then the Little People.

If the child has difficulty, ask if you may assist.

Repeat the activity and let the child help mix up the toys.

Take one of the toy cars and place it with the kitchen; ask the child if this is correct.

Repeat the activity with some of the other toys.

Fine Motor Skills

Activity: Coloring

Goal: Develop fine motor skills and color recognition

Supplies:

- ✓ Favorite character coloring book
- ✓ Washable crayons, regular size (other crayons can be difficult for younger children)
- ✓ Child's small table and chairs
- ✓ Plain paper or construction paper

Implementation:

Place the child at the table with his favorite character coloring book and 2-3 crayons.

Sit down with the child and color the picture with the child; one portion of the page will be colored by the caregiver and the other portion will be colored by the child.

Coloring with the child allows demonstration of the proper way to color and stay within the lines.

Describe each portion of the page the child is coloring.

Describe each color the child is using.

Another color idea (if the child knows colors) is to create your own color by number using color by picture.

Look through the coloring books and identify themes. Example: If the coloring book has several flowers, dogs and cats, all flowers will be red, all cats will be yellow and all dogs will be brown (use primary colors only).

Ask the child to color the flower in the designated picture red.

Ask the child to color the cat in the designated picture yellow.

Ask the child to color the dog in the designated picture brown.

If the child has difficulty, do not allow him to get frustrated; assist him with locating the correct color and picture.

Additional activities would be:

Have the child draw his version of a dog, house or flower on a plain piece of paper.

Have the child color the drawing and ask the child what colors he is using.

Fine Motor Skills

Activity: Folding

Goal: Develop fine motor skills through the folding motions

Supplies:

- ✓ Tissue wrapping paper, notebook paper, dish towels
- ✓ Child's small table and chairs

Implementation:

Place the child at the table in the chair.

Have several pieces of notebook paper, tissue wrapping paper, and square dish towels on the table.

Take the piece of paper and fold it in half, moving downward.

Have the child take a piece of paper and fold it in half, moving downward (describe the process during each step).

Next, fold the caregiver's paper in half again, moving downward.

Have the child fold her piece of paper in half again, moving downward.

Each time, describe the process of folding using your hands and making the paper smaller.

Repeat the above process with the tissue wrapping paper and the dish towel.

Afterward, take another piece of paper, tissue wrapping paper and a dish towel.

Fold each item two or three times.

Hand the item to the child and request that she unfold each item.

After the child unfolds each item, work with her to see if she can fold each item back into its proper form.

Fine Motor Skills

Activity: Cutting with safety scissors

Goal: Developing fine motor skills including manual dexterity

Supplies:

- ✓ Coloring book or old magazines
- ✓ Pair of child safety scissors
- ✓ Child's table and chairs
- ✓ Piece of plain paper with straight line drawn
- ✓ Work tray

Implementation:

Place the coloring books, magazines and scissors into the work tray and place on the table.

Let the child assist you with removing all objects from the tray; as each object is removed, describe the object to the child.

Pick up the coloring book and tear a page from the book.

Cut the page into 4 pieces while the child is watching.

Ask the child if she would like to try.

Leave the child to complete the activity without the caregiver at the table (observe from a distance).

Give the child a few minutes and if the child does not begin the activity, ask the child if you may assist.

Guide the child as needed with the scissors and cutting the pages; remove your guiding hand if the child does not require assistance.

Show the child how to place the pieces back together similar to a puzzle.

Ask the child to place the pieces back together and make his own puzzle.

After the child has mastered this skill, you may move on to cutting different textures such as felt, construction paper, other cloth.

Another idea is to take the piece of paper with the line and cut the line.

Use another piece of paper with a line and have the child try to cut on the line.

Fine Motor Skills

Activity: Stacking objects

Goal: Develop fine motor skills

Supplies:

- ✓ Stackable cups (6-10)
- ✓ Blocks (15-20)
- ✓ Shoe boxes (5 or 6)
- ✓ Books
- ✓ Tray

Implementation:

Have the child sit at the table and bring the tray filled with stackable blocks (small wooden blocks work best).

Tell the child to stack the blocks and build a tall tower, as tall as possible; if needed, ask the child if he requires help.

Demonstrate how to stack the blocks into a tall tower and then knock the blocks down.

Repeat the activity.

Take 5 or 6 shoe boxes and show the child how to stack them on top of each other to build a tall tower.

Encourage the child to build a house or other simple structure; take 5 blocks and place 3 blocks apart; show the child how to add the other two blocks on top and in between the other blocks.

Have the child stack the shoe boxes and then knock them all down.

Take the stackable cups or plastic drinking cups and turn them upside down.

Have the child stack the cups and knock them down.

Let the child choose her favorite book with thick pages.

Have the child come to the center of the floor and sit with her legs crossed.

Tell the child it is time for story-time, and the child will be helping.

Start reading the story and have the child turn the page when indicated.

Fine Motor Skills

Activity: Choo Choo Train

Goal: Develop fine motor skills

Supplies:

- ✓ Shoe boxes (3)
- ✓ White paper or white wrapping paper
- ✓ Tape
- ✓ String, Shoe strings or ribbon
- ✓ Hole punch
- ✓ Crayons and washable markers
- ✓ Card board
- ✓ Child's small table and chairs
- ✓ Basket for supplies

Implementation:

Have the table prepared with a shoe box and bring the following items in a basket: tape, white paper.

Ask the child to sit down and tell her you are going to make a choo choo train.

Take the shoe boxes and wrap them in white paper like a present; ask the child to assist by folding the paper over the box and holding while you tape the box.

Repeat the procedure for the remaining two boxes.

Take all of the boxes away except one.

Provide the child with crayons or washable markers and ask her to decorate the box; let her decorate in any way she chooses.

Repeat the procedure for the remaining boxes.

After each box has been completed, get the hole punch and punch a hole in each box in the front center and back center.

Have the child take the string, shoe strings or ribbon and thread through the holes in each box. Assist if needed.

In the last box, tie a knot at the end of the string, shoe string or ribbon.

Now, with all boxes connected, encourage the child to leave the table and pull the train.

Emphasize what a great toy that the child has created.

Fine Motor Skills Game

Activity: Art project

Goal: Fine Motor and Personal-Social Skills

Supplies:

- ✓ Construction paper and children's glue stick
- ✓ Magazines with pictures
- ✓ Colored yarn
- ✓ Crayons and/or washable markers
- ✓ Child's small table and chairs
- ✓ Safety scissors
- ✓ Stickers
- ✓ Cardboard box with a lid (example: copier paper box)

Implementation:

Place all items listed above into the cardboard box with a lid.

Place the box in the middle of the floor.

Tell the child he is going to create his very own keepsake box.

Tell the child he will decorate the box any way that he chooses with the items found inside the box.

Move away from the child and let him explore the items inside the box.

Afterward, name each item that was inside the box.

Ask the child to pick one thing he would like to use to decorate the box.

Assist the child as required with the item he has chosen. (Example: Open stickers, or if the child chooses construction paper, ask him what she would like to make.)

Let the child cut the construction paper in any fashion that he likes; if the child cannot use safety scissors, ask him if you may assist and ask the child what he would like you to make for him.

After the child completes the preparation for the first item chosen, show the child how to place the item on the box.

After the item is placed on the box, let the child choose another item.

Assist the child with ideas, but let him be the creative genius for the box.

Let the child know that this is his box and he can decorate in any way he chooses.

After all the items inside the box have been used and the box is complete, allow everything to settle and dry on the box.

Later in the afternoon, bring the box back out and ask the child what he would like to place in box.

Help the child fill the box with his favorite things.

Fine Motor Skills Game

Activity: Fun with painting

Goal: Fine Motor and Language skills

Supplies:

- ✓ Finger paint (red, blue, yellow, green) and/or chocolate pudding
- ✓ Plastic plate and/or poster board
- ✓ Paper towels
- ✓ Sponge alphabet letters and numbers
- ✓ 2 Shower curtain liners or child's food drop cloth
- ✓ Old clothes and/or painting smock
- ✓ Child's small table and chairs

Implementation:

This game can be completed inside with a little preparation or works well outside. If you choose to complete this game inside, make sure you have the activity in only one area that is not carpeted.

Inside:

Take a shower curtain liner and place underneath the child's table, as well a shower curtain liner on top of the table.

Place the paint or pudding in small plastic containers and put each paint container on the table.

Have the child join you at the small table and sit in the chair.

Tell her you are going to play a game with fingers and finger paint.

Take the child's forefinger and lightly place it into the paint or pudding.

Let the child rub the paint or pudding in his hand and between her fingers to get used to the texture.

Describe the feel of the paint and ask the child what the paint is like, (Example: "Is it cold, smooth, wet, squishy?")

Show the child how to draw and make marks on the poster board or a plate with the paint.

Allow the child to experiment with the paint and draw on the poster board.

Wipe the child's hands and start the game.

Tell the child the rules of the game:

- ✓ The caregiver will give you a command.
- ✓ The child puts on his listening ears and follows the command.
- ✓ If the child needs assistance, he may ask for help.

Begin by giving the child an example of the game.

Caregiver: Draw several letters in several different colors on the poster board.

Child: Child is asked to put his finger in the green paint and place a mark underneath the blue A.

Continue alternating letters and describe the sound each letter makes.

Pudding is an alternate if you do not have paint, but pudding will only be one color, so letters will have to be reviewed without the colors.

Another alternative is to use the sponge alphabet letters.

Have the child choose a letter; name the letter and the color of the letter.

Ask the child to place the letter in one of the paint containers, then place the letter on the poster board.

Repeat with several letters and numbers.

CreativCare Learning Guides

Fine Motor Skills Game

Activity: Sand Play

Goal: Fine Motor and Personal-Social Skills

Supplies:

- ✓ Play Sand
- ✓ Sand and water table or homemade table (wagon and clear Rubbermaid containers)
- ✓ Boat, water toy cups

Implementation:

Tell the child that today we will be playing with sand and water.

Use a sand or water table or create a sand and water table by using a pull wagon and clear Rubbermaid containers. The beauty of creating your own sand and water table is that the wagon can be pulled to different locations in the yard.

After arranging the table, place water in one side and sand in the other side.

Ask the child to place a boat in the water and the toy cups in the sand.

Show the child how the boat moves along the water and how to fill the cups with water and sand.

Talk with the child about filling and emptying the containers.

Introduce building a sand castle and how the water changes the sands consistency.

Allow the child free time to experiment and explore the sand and water.

Show the child how the boat can go under and over a bridge.

Continue free play, which allows for the ultimate learning experience.

Gross Motor Skills

Activity: Play Ball

Goal: Develop Gross Motor Skills

Supplies:

- ✓ Nerf ball or small soft ball
- ✓ Plastic tub
- ✓ Bucket or basket
- ✓ Colored masking tape

Implementation:

Have the child gather the Nerf balls into the bucket or basket.

Assist the child and take the bucket to one corner of the room.

Provide the child with a 3 inch strip of the colored tape.

Move the child back approximately 2.5 feet and have her press the tape on the floor.

Request that the child gather the Nerf balls, place them in the basket and bring him behind the tape; place the balls on the floor in a straight line.

Demonstrate to the child how to throw the balls into the basket one by one.

When the bucket is missed, gather the balls and place them into the basket.

Take all of the missed balls and place them into the bucket.

Place the child behind the line with the basket of balls and see if he begins the activity; if not offer to assist.

An alternative to this activity, after this is mastered, would be to get a Nerf basketball set and have her practice hitting the hoop.

Another alternative is a game of simple catch.

Gross Motor Skills

Activity: Outside Fun - Let's Run

Goal: Develop gross motor skills

Supplies:

- ✓ Backyard or park
- ✓ Large ball

Implementation:

Take the child outside or to a park in a large open grassy space.

Tell the child that outside time today will include running and jumping.

Place a large ball several feet away.

Take the child to the starting point and tell him to run as fast as he can to get the ball.

Next, ask the child to touch the ball and run back to the caregiver.

Repeat this sequence several times.

Remind the child each time that we run outdoors and not inside.

Take the child back to the original starting point and tell him you are going to play a jumping game.

Demonstrate how to jump and then describe the game.

Pick a song that is interactive, such as an animal song, and sing about an animal that jumps (example: a bunny).

Every time you say "jump," the child must jump or try to jump.

Demonstrate when to jump for the child, then complete the activity together.

If you do not know a song, make a song up to the "Row, Row, Row, Your Boat" theme.

Example: "Jump, Jump, Jump, my bunny as fast as you can merrily, merrily merrily, merrily all the way home again."

Gross Motor Skills

Activity: Bottle Bowling

Goal: Gross Motor Skills and Hand-eye coordination

Supplies:

- ✓ Ball (approximately the size of a Nerf ball)
- ✓ Plastic soda bottles (10)
- ✓ Colored tape

Implementation:

Have the child assist you with gathering the necessary equipment; the child can carry the ball and tape.

Find a room with lots of space.

Have the child place a piece of the colored tape on the floor.

March approximately 4 feet forward; place the soda bottles with the following arrangement: 4 pins in back, 3 pins in front of the 4, 2 pins in front of the 3, and 1 in front of 2 pins.

Have the child go back to the tape.

Demonstrate how to roll the ball to knock over the soda bottles.

Afterward, reset the soda bottles and have the child try to knock over the soda bottles.

Have the child count the number of bottles knocked down and the number of bottles that remain standing.

Continue the activity and demonstrate as often as needed.

Praise the child each time he tries to knock over the bottles.

Gross Motor Skills

Activity: Slide time

Goal: Gross motor skills

Supplies:

- ✓ Backyard or playground
- ✓ Medium slide with ladder
- ✓ Stuffed animal or doll

Implementation:

Take the child outside or to the nearest playground.

On the way outside or to the playground, discuss the activities that the child will be doing.

Talk about the swings, teeter totter and save the slide for last.

Discuss the concepts of going up the ladder and down the slide.

Have the child's stuffed animal or doll pretend to go up the ladder, sit down and slide down the slide several times.

Next, encourage the child to climb the ladder with your help; start at the bottom rung and alternate the child's feet up the ladder.

If the child is confident and it is safe, allow the child to climb the ladder without the caregivers help (always stay right behind the child in case he slips).

Repeat these steps several times until the child is comfortable; never force the child to climb.

If the child is not interested, allow her to play on other equipment and come back to the slide later.

Once the child masters climbing, have her sit and slide down the slide.

The caregiver should be at the bottom of the slide to catch the child.

Repeat the procedure again.

Gross Motor Skills

Activity: Dance to the music

Goal: Gross motor skills

Supplies:

- ✓ CD with dance songs (children's songs are best) or just sing
- ✓ Comfortable clothes that move

Implementation:

Tell the child today is Dance Day; you will be listening to music and moving your body with the music.

Turn on the CD player and start the music; show the child how to move your arms and legs, bend over, turnaround, etc. to dance.

Tell the child to do a specific activity, which is associated with a specific portion of the song; demonstrate twice and then have the child do the activities with you and eventually alone.

Example: "How Much Is That Doggie In The Window?"

Song Actions:

"How much is that doggie in the window? (Body swaying back and forth Bark, Bark, Clap, Clap); The one with the waggley tail" (Shake your hips).

Repeat as the words repeat.

Example: "London Bridges Falling Down"

Song Actions:

"London Bridges (make a triangle by holding hands up high and letting the fingertips touch); falling down, falling down, falling down (release fingertips and let hands drop); My fair lady." Repeat previous words and actions.

"Take the key and lock her up" (intertwine hands and fingers and sway arms back and forth). Repeat words and actions.

Example: "Twinkle, Twinkle, Little Star"

"Twinkle Twinkle (take all four fingers and bring them into the thumb, similar to making a mouth movement with your hands; raise your hands in the air completing the mouth-like movement); little star how I wonder what you are; up above the world so high (raise hands above head and stretch arms outward); like a diamond in the sky" (place two thumbs and forefingers together to make a diamond). Repeat the words and actions.

The next activity should be free movement through dance.

Show the child how to dance to the music using all body parts; this is great fun and wonderful exercise.

Gross Motor Skills Game

Activity: Animal Music

Goal: Develop Gross Motor Skills and Music Appreciation

Supplies:

- ✓ Animal sounds CD
- ✓ Large open space

Implementation:

Find an animal sounds CD or animal sounds and movement CD

Demonstrate one by one how to move and sound similar to the specific animal.

Example:

If there is an elephant, you would bring your arms down low, lock your hands together with a swinging motion back and forth, and make an elephant sound.

Walk around swinging your trunk like an elephant.

Next, ask the child to pretend to walk like an elephant.

If the child is having difficulty, ask if you may assist and show her the process again.

Continue with the elephant for several minutes.

Move to the next animal

Example:

You can pretend that you are a bunny and hop like a bunny (hopping will be a difficult, concept but the child can try at this age).

Put your feet together and jump, singing "hop, hop, hop like a bunny."

After you demonstrate, have the child try.

You can continue with any animal.

A few favorites are an alligator, cat, or turtle.

Use animals that have different speeds to work on the concepts of slow and fast.

Vary the animals, such as the bunny and then the turtle.

Gross Motor Skills Game

Activity: Obstacle Course

Goal: Develop Gross Motor Skills and Cognitive Skills

Supplies:

- ✓ Jump ropes or ribbons
- ✓ Child's tunnel
- ✓ Cardboard boxes
- ✓ Ball

Implementation:

Set up a toddler obstacle course with the items listed above. If you do not have a child's tunnel, use the kitchen table.

Place a child's jump rope or ribbon on the floor.

Place a child's tunnel on the floor.

Place a large cardboard box on the floor.

Place a medium-size ball on the floor.

Begin by jumping or stepping over the rope/ribbon.

Next, climb on the couch and sit down.

Next, go through the tunnel (or under the table).

Next, go to the box and step into the box or sit on the box (depending on how sturdy the box is).

The final obstacle is to get the ball and roll it to a specific point.

Demonstrate each obstacle one by one.

Then demonstrate again.

Afterward, let the child try each obstacle one by one.

The child must master each obstacle before moving on to the next one.

If the child is having difficulty, ask if you may assist.

Repeat this procedure several times.

Gross Motor Skills Game

Activity: Scenario

Goal: Develop Gross Motor Skills

Supplies:

- ✓ Paper and pencil
- ✓ Dora the Explorer episode (optional)

Implementation:

Write scenarios (plays) with movement activities in the scenarios (If the parent agrees, you can just use a Dora episode).

If not, here is an example of a scenario:

"Dora or Diego are going camping and they are taking lots of supplies." (Reach down and gather your supplies; show the child the motion of bending down and pretending to place items in a container for the trip.)

"Now everything is all packed, and we need to load the car." (Twist at the waist, side to side as if loading the car; show the child the motions.)

"Now, drive the car to the camp site." (Sit on the floor or couch and bring your arms and hands up like you are driving; show the child the motions.)

You can complete the scenario in another lesson because the above is probably enough to do for one session.

Day Two

"We have arrived at the campsite and there are turtles in the road; we need to step or jump over the turtles."

Demonstrate how to jump or step over the turtles.

"Now you need to swing across the lake."

Pretend to grab a rope hanging from the trees and swing.

Show the child the motions.

Make sure to demonstrate everything first.

You can continue with this scenario or create additional scenarios.

Again, an option with parent approval, is to use a Dora or Diego episode.

Language Skills

Activity: Reading

Goal: Develop Receptive and Expressive Language

Supplies:

✓ Child's favorite board books (3 books)

Implementation

Sit with the child on the floor, or couch with 3 or his favorite books.

It is story-time; he will choose which book he would like to read first.

Example: Dora the Explorer book

Start the story by asking the child which characters are on the front page.

Point to the book and ask, "Which one is Dora? Which one is Boots?"

Ask the child to pick out something red in the picture.

Follow this by asking for something blue, then yellow and then green

Ask the child what activities the characters are doing.

Move to the next page in the book.

Read the words on the page.

After reading the words, describe what is on the page.

Ask the child who is wearing red; ask the child to identify something red.

Next, ask the child to identify something blue, yellow, and then green.

Ask the child if he sees any other colors.

Ask the child what the characters on the page are doing.

Repeat this process with each page.

After the last page has been read and described;

Ask the child to read the book.

The child will make up her language; do not interrupt this process.

Repeat all procedures for the next two books.

CreativCare Learning Guides

Language Skills

Activity: What does this do?

Goal: Develop Receptive and Expressive Language

Supplies:

- ✓ Cup
- ✓ Bath cloth
- ✓ Ball
- ✓ Learning Basket
- ✓ Child's small table and chair

Implementation

Ask the child to sit at her table and bring the Learning Basket with all the above items.

Take the cup out of the basket and state, "this is a cup;" ask the child how we use a cup.

Take the bath cloth out of the Learning Basket and state, "this is a bath cloth;" ask the child how we use a bath cloth.

Take the ball out of the Learning Basket and state, "this is ball;" ask the child how we use the ball.

Place the items back into Learning Basket.

Pull the ball out of the basket and ask the child how we use the ball.

Next, pull the cup out of the basket and ask the child how we use the cup.

Pull the bath cloth out of the Learning Basket and ask the child how we use the bath cloth.

Afterward, arrange the three items in a row.

Ask the child to choose the item that helps us drink.

Place the cup back in the row and rearrange the placement of the items.

Ask the child to choose the item that helps us stay clean.

Put the bath cloth back in the row and rearrange the area of the cloth

Ask the child to choose the item that helps us play.

Repeat the activity and after the activity is mastered, add another item.

Eventually, add all new items.

CreativCare Learning Guides

Language Skills

Activity: Up, Down, and All Around

Goal: Develop Receptive Language through directional words

Supplies:

- ✓ Books or pictures of directional words
- ✓ May utilize Complimentary Coloring Book for some of the words *Things I Want to Know at Three*
- ✓ Child's small table and chairs
- ✓ Learning Basket
- ✓ Key ring or notecard ring
- ✓ Hole punch
- ✓ Construction paper
- ✓ Glue

Implementation

If you choose not to utilize the Complimentary Coloring Book listed above, find pictures that contain the following directional words:

Up, Down, Over, Under, Above, Beside, In Front of, Behind, In, On

Cut out pictures of magazines or coloring books that demonstrate all of the above directional terms.

Using the construction paper, cut 5 pages into halves.

Take the pictures chosen and glue 1 picture to half a piece of construction paper.

Suggestion: Use many colors of construction paper so you can remind the child of her colors during this activity.

Punch a hole in the corner of each half of construction paper and place the construction paper with the directional word picture on a key ring or notecard ring.

This forms your directional word book.

Place your word book and/or the *Things I Want to Know at Three* Coloring Book into the learning tray.

Have the child sit at her small table while you place the Learning Basket beside the child.

Tell her you will be looking at pictures of directions.

Show the child the first picture and describe the picture using direction

For Example: In the coloring book, the picture is a fish **in** a bowl.

Explain that there is a bowl and the fish is **in** the bowl.

If the fish were to jump out of the bowl, the fish would be **out** and not **in**

Move on to the next picture and repeat the same procedure.

Continue going through the pictures.

After the child has a better grasp, ask the child which picture shows **out**

Next, ask the child which picture shows **in**. Continue the process.

CreativCare Learning Guides

Language Skills

Activity: Size

Goal: Develop Receptive and Expressive Language

Supplies:

- ✓ Several objects of different sizes showing big and little
- ✓ Learning Basket

Implementation

Place several objects of different sizes into the Learning Basket

Ask the child to join you on the floor.

Take 2 objects from the basket, one large and one small.

Ex: baby cup and adult cup

Place the cups side by side and touch the small cup; tell the child, "this cup is small."

Place the cups side by side and touch the large cup; tell the child, "this cup is large."

Place the cups side by side and ask the child to point to the small cup.

Place the cups side by side and ask the child to point to the large cup.

Other examples would be a baby shoe and an adult shoe or books of different sizes.

Continue this process throughout the day, pointing out objects of different size.

Tell the child that you are large and he is small.

Another avenue would be to describe what the objects you are using do, such as, "we use cups to drink."

Ask the child to go around the room and point to small objects and then point to large objects.

Language Skills

Activity: Talk, Talk, Talk

Goal: Language skills

Supplies:

- ✓ Driving in the car to the park

Implementation:

When you take the child on trips to the store or park, describe everything you see and do.

Start by telling the child what the activity is for the day.

Example: Trip to the park

"Today, we are going to get into the car and drive to the park."

"We are getting into the red car, and the seats are tan. We are going to put you into your seat so you will be safe."

"We are driving down the road that is black with yellow lines."

"Here is a stoplight; a red light means stop, so we stop our car."

"The green light means go, and we can start driving"

"The yellow light means slow down."

"A brown dog and a white cat are in the yard. What does the dog say and what does the cat say?"

"We are almost at the park; we just passed a school."

"Now that we are at the park, let's take a walk."

"Look, the boy is playing with a red ball."

"The little girl is playing with a pink car."

"There are flowers with white petals."

"See the green bushes."

"What is that little girl doing? Is she swinging?"

"Can you show me the yellow flower?"

Every place that you go and everything that you do with the child, describe, describe, describe.

Language Skills Game

Activity: What does this do?

Goal: Receptive Language skills

Supplies:

- ✓ Construction paper and glue
- ✓ Picture of a cup
- ✓ Picture of a fork
- ✓ Picture of a coat
- ✓ Picture of a chair
- ✓ Picture of a ball
- ✓ Learning tray

Implementation:

Cut out pictures and paste them individually on a piece of construction paper.

Place the pictures in the learning tray.

Ask the child to join you in the center of the floor.

Tell the child you are going to play a game.

Explain the rules of the game.

Rule 1: Pick a picture out of the learning tray.

Rule 2: The caregiver will ask what the use of the item is.

If the child does not know, give her a hint.

Example:

The child pulls out the cup.

"How do we use this object?"

The child says "no" or he doesn't know.

Caregiver response: "When we have breakfast, we use the cup to hold our milk and to _____." (mimic a drinking motion)

If the child still does not know, tell him we use a cup to drink.

Follow each step above for each object chosen from the Learning Basket

After all pictures of the items have been removed from the Learning Basket, place the pictures back into the basket; mix up the pictures and start the game again.

Language Skills Game

Activity: Sing a Song

Goal: Develop language skills

Supplies:

- ✓ Lyrics to "The Bear"
- ✓ Lyrics to "Teddy Bear, Teddy Bear"
- ✓ Lyrics to "London Bridges"
- ✓ Lyrics to "Twinkle, Twinkle, Little Star"
- ✓ Teddy bear

Implementation:

Start by singing each song through several times during the day; you may use CDs, but still make sure you are singing the words along with the CD.

After several repetitions, the child will probably start singing along as well.

The child may make up her own words; encourage the child to say the words and praise her for making up her own words.

Continue this process until the child is more comfortable with the song.

After the child is trying to sing the song all the way through, add some motions.

Example:

"The Bear"

Motions:

- ✓ Use a teddy bear to complete the motions
- ✓ Take the teddy bear up into the air and then down for "going over the mountain."
- ✓ Place your hands above the teddy bear's eyes for "see what he could see."
- ✓ Repeat the motions
- ✓ Let the child use the bear and repeat the motions.

"Teddy Bear, Teddy Bear"

Motions:

- ✓ Use a teddy bear and turn around in circles with the bear for the turnaround portion of the song.
- ✓ Touch the floor with the bear.
- ✓ Bring one foot of the teddy bear forward for show your shoe or foot.
- ✓ Let the teddy bear crawl through a tunnel or your legs.
- ✓ Repeat the motions.
- ✓ Let the child use the bear and repeat the motions.

CreativCare Learning Guides

Try letting the child complete the motions rather than having the teddy bear complete the motions.

Let the child make up new verses and actions with the song.

Language Skills Game

Activity: Making a Book

Goal: Language and Fine Motor Skills

Supplies:

- ✓ Construction paper and children's glue stick
- ✓ Magazines with pictures
- ✓ Hole punch
- ✓ Colored yarn
- ✓ Learning Tray
- ✓ Crayons
- ✓ Child's small table and Chairs
- ✓ Safety scissors

Implementation:

Prepare the construction paper by punching 3 holes along one side.

Pre-cut the yarn: three strips about 6 inches long each.

Place all items in the Learning Basket.

Ask the child to join you at the table.

Tell the child you will be making a book.

Show the child the magazines and tell her to only play with the magazines she is given.

Ask the child to go through the magazine and pick out a picture she would like to use in her book.

Leave the table and give the child some space to choose a picture.

If the child is having difficulty, ask if you may assist.

After the child chooses a picture, ask her what is in the picture.

Help the child to cut around the picture.

Next, ask the child to pick a color of construction paper and put some glue on the page.

Give the child some space to complete this task.

Afterward, tell the child to place her picture on the construction paper on top of the glue.

Continue this process with 5-10 pictures.

After all pictures are glued on the page, go back and discuss each picture chosen.

Assist the child to write the name of the picture on the bottom of the page by asking the child to hold her crayon; take your hand around the child's to write the letters of the words.

Use different color crayons.

After each picture has been named, show the child how to organize the pictures into a book.

Show the child how to take a piece of yarn and place it through the holes.

Tie the yarn in a knot and then into a bow.

Repeat the procedure with the other two holes. Sit on the floor with the child and look at her book.

Personal-Social Skills

Activity: Dressing

Goal: Developing autonomy and self-help skills

Supplies:

- ✓ Dress up doll with removable clothing: buttons, ties, velcro, zippers, shoes
- ✓ 2 sets of child's clothes and shoes
- ✓ Optional: cloth with button and button hole; cloth with zipper, cloth with velcro
- ✓ Optional: getting dressed song

Implementation:

Begin by talking to the child and telling her each step of the way what you are doing (Example: "We are going to pick out your clothes now"); toddlers need repetition

Allow the child to pick out her clothes, giving her a choice of 2 sets of clothing that you have chosen.

Work with the child when putting on clothes, providing her with which leg or arm you are putting into the clothes and making sure to hold her hands up when putting a shirt over her head.

Utilize a dress up doll with zippers, ties, velcro, and buttons.

CreativCare Learning Guides

Have the child undress the doll, describing each step as she tries to untie the shoe, unzip the coat; remove the velcro from the shoe, etc.

Another idea is to make cloth with zippers, buttons, and velcro.

Personal-Social Skills

Activity: Meal-time

Goal: Developing autonomy and self-help skills

Supplies:

- ✓ Small child's table and chair
- ✓ Cabinets arranged with plates, cups, and spoons on the lower level
- ✓ Child's utensils
- ✓ Cookie cutters

Implementation:

All of the child's meals should be at the small table. This provides the child with some control, as well as placing the food, utensils, dishes and cups on her own level.

All plates, cups, utensils and bowls should be located on the child's level, using the lower cabinet or shelf in the home.

Prepare nutritious meals for the child including a fruit, vegetable, bread and meat or protein.

Allow the child to have a choice of what to eat, but give only 2 options.

After the meal is ready, have the child go to the cabinet and get her plate, cup, fork/spoon, and napkin.

Take the plate from the child and place the food on the tray; be creative with her food (example: broccoli becomes little trees, a peanut butter sandwich becomes whatever shape you like using a cookie cutter); always vary color and texture.

Have the child sit at the table and then you place the plate of food in front of her.

Make sure to talk about the colors and shapes of the food, but do not bribe. Tell the child that she needs to eat or make a big deal out of the food in order to encourage her.

This age group can be very picky and eat very little for the most part.

Food is also the way that this age group tries to control, so do not make a big deal out of eating; place the food in front of the child without a lot of commentary.

Personal-Social Skills

Activity: Feelings and Interpretation

Goal: Recognize Basic Emotions

Supplies:

- ✓ Magazine cut-out of people showing the following emotions: happy, sad, fear, anger, excitement
- ✓ Felt cut-outs (large round circles, small round circles for nose, mouths - turning up, down, exaggerated upward showing teeth)
- ✓ Construction paper
- ✓ Child's glue
- ✓ Scissors
- ✓ Movable stuffed animal or doll eyes
- ✓ Children's book about emotion

Implementation:

Read a short children's book about emotions, pointing out each emotion.

Make a collage of the magazine pictures on construction paper using 1-2 pictures of each emotion An alternative would be to glue the people showing emotion onto a popsicle stick.

Review each emotion with the child by pointing to one magazine picture of happy and one picture of sad; ask the child which person is happy and then ask the child to point to the picture of the person who is sad; repeat for each emotion.

Make faces using felt by gluing the small circles and mouths on the large circle for the face; add movable eyes.

Show the child each face; place each face side by side and ask the child to point to the face that is happy, sad, etc.

Personal-Social Skills

Activity: Let's pretend

Goal: Imagination Development

Supplies:

- ✓ Child's toy that has a house or car and Fisher Price Little People or animals
- ✓ Building blocks
- ✓ Baby doll
- ✓ Child's kitchen set with play food

Implementation:

Place the house or car along with the Little People in the middle of the room.

Sit down with the child and the toys.

Use blocks to build a house or use the playhouse that is already onsite.

Use household furniture or doll beds to play house.

Play with the child, showing her how to pretend using the following scenarios:

- ❖ Pretend you are the mommy or daddy and this is the baby, and they are getting into the minivan to drive to the store.

❖ Take one of the Little People or animals and have her ring the doorbell of the house to enter; pretend that the Little Person has come by to visit and provide her with a snack and drink.

❖ Use the building blocks to build an ice cream shop or grocery store.

❖ Ask the child to cook you a hamburger, eggs or whatever type of play food she has available; show the child how to beat the eggs or flip the hamburger.

❖ Have the child set the play table for you.

❖ Play house with the child and his/her doll or animal.

Personal-Social Skills

Activity: Walking through the backyard or park

Goal: Developing a sense of self and the environment

Supplies:

- ✓ Backyard or a park
- ✓ Pictures in a book or magazine of nature (flowers, trees, grass, bees, bugs, etc.)
- ✓ Tricycle or ride-on toy
- ✓ Swing

Implementation:

During morning time, sit with the child on the floor and show her the pictures you have located of nature.

Describe each picture using texture, color, smell, size.

Point to each object.

Name each object and have the child name them back.

Advise the child that during outside time, you will be identifying the objects that the child saw in the picture.

Review the pictures again, repeating all of the above directions.

During the afternoon, take the child outside or to the park and start identifying as many objects in the picture as possible.

Continue to walk around the yard and identify objects, animals, bugs, etc.

With everything you see, describe the objects' color, texture, smell, and size.

Try to take walks daily as weather allows. It is important for a child to realize her environment encompasses everything around her.

During outside time, incorporate other activities such as swinging, riding a tricycle or other activities that the child especially enjoys.

Describe each activity fully as the child participates.

Personal-Social Skills Game

Activity: Can't Find Me

Goal: Personal-Social and Cognitive Skills Enhancement

Supplies:

✓ Stuffed animal to hide or Hallmark's Hide and Seek Bunny

Implementation:

Ask the child to join you on the floor

Talk with the child about the thrill of hiding an object and then someone else finding that object.

Explain the game of hide and seek to the child.

Start by demonstrating for the child how to play the game.

Next, ask the child to cover her eyes; you may need to demonstrate what covering your eyes really means.

If you have the Hide and Seek Bunny, use the bunny to assist in hide and seek before moving to an animal that does not speak.

The bunny is activated when his hat is moved downward; the bunny speaks during the game saying things such as, "I'm hiding now."

If you do not have the bunny or something similar, simply begin with hiding a regular animal.

Hide the animal, and then show the child how to search for the missing animal.

Talk with the child about what it means to be warmer and colder (this is a higher level concept but worth mentioning).

Allow the child to hide the animal and you search.

Continue this process, hiding different objects.

This is an excellent game to enhance personal-social skills when friends come to play.

Personal-Social Skills Game

Activity: Nice to Meet You

Goal: Role playing and Social Skills

Supplies:

- ✓ Room with 3 stuffed animals or dolls
- ✓ Puzzle

Implementation:

Have the child choose 3 stuffed animals or dolls and place them in different locations in the room.

Tell the child you will be playing pretend classroom.

Demonstrate the following for the child:

Walk up to the first animal or doll and say, "Hi my name is (your name); what is your name?"

Ask the animal or doll, "How are you doing today?"

"Would you like to play puzzles?"

Retrieve one of the puzzles and place it in front of the doll or animal.

Put the puzzle together, all while talking to the animal or doll.

Have the doll or animal speak back to you.

Afterwards, let the child follow the same instructions you followed above.

Provide different scenarios with each doll or animal.

A few examples are:

- ❖ Mealtime
- ❖ Story time
- ❖ Playing with a ball

During all scenarios, the child should be talking to the doll or animal and the doll or animal should be speaking back to the child.

The scenarios will assist the child in learning to interact with others, to share, and to have conversations, all while using pretend play.

CreativCare Learning Guides

Personal-Social Skills Game

Activity: Puppet Time

Goal: Role playing and Social Skills

Supplies:

- ✓ Two puppets
- ✓ Puppet show or write your own puppet show
- ✓ Puppet theater, cardboard box

Implementation:

Have the child sit on the floor and tell her to wait and some new friends who will be coming by to see her.

Set up the puppet theater with whatever you have at your disposal that will allow you to be hidden, with the exception of your puppet hands. You can use a large box or hide behind a chair.

Use a prepared puppet show or the puppet show that you have written.

An example of a show is listed below:

Friendship

Puppets: Leo the Lion and Oliver the Owl

"Today we are going to learn about friendship. Ready, Set, Go!"

Leo: "Hi Oliver! How are you?"

Oliver: "Fine! What's going on with you?"

Leo: "We have some new neighbors moving in. There's a little boy my age. My mom wants me to meet him."

Oliver: "That's nice. Why don't you want to meet him?"

Leo: "I have enough friends. I don't need another one."

Oliver: "We can always use more friends. You can never have too many!"

Leo: "Well, he did have some nice toys I saw."

Oliver: "Friendship isn't about toys. It's about caring and being there for each other in good times and bad."

Leo: "You are so wise, Oliver. I'll go over and make a new friend."

You can use any puppet show that demonstrates social skills.

Chapter 6: Three to Five Years

Preschoolers demonstrate the following abilities: sitting still for several minutes, playing with others, knowing prepositions, singing all the verses of songs and drawing shapes. The preschooler is trying to gain the skills to be ready for school.

The top four skills for this age group are the following:

- ❖ Knows ABCs and 123s; answers questions
- ❖ Can catch, hit and kick a ball; climbs and jumps
- ❖ Can draw a person and a house; uses scissors
- ❖ Gets dressed, including buttons, snaps, zippers, etc.

The top four educational toys for this age group are the following:

- ❖ Play set including slide
- ❖ Children's tablet (Innotab or Leap Pad)
- ❖ Ready to Read Book
- ❖ Dress up Doll

CreativCare Learning Guides

CreativCare Services Milestones (3-5 Years)

	Developmental Category	Developmental Milestones
☐	Language	Understands present and future tenses
☐		Forms 5-6 word sentences
☐		Constantly asks questions
☐		Says ABCs and counts to 20
☐		Follows 3 unrelated commands
☐		Understands comparatives
☐		Uses words can, will, shall and might
☐		Speaks grammatically proper
☐	Motor	Bends and touches toes without bending knees
☐		Plays many types of ball
☐		Climbs, slides and swings
☐		Balances on 1 foot
☐		Uses scissors to cut paper and can cut on a straight line
☐		Copies letters, shapes and numbers
☐		Draws a person with at least 6 body parts
☐		Draws a house with features (door, chimney, roof)

NOTE: All children develop at different rates. The above milestones are general guidelines for children's development. Some children are advanced in specific areas and behind in others. Consult your child's Pediatrician if there are questions or concerns.

CreativCare Services Milestones (3-5 Years)

	Developmental Category	Developmental Milestones
☐	Cognitive	Understands plurals
☐		Responds to simple logic questions
☐		Completes 10 piece puzzles; 5 year olds can complete 30 piece large puzzles
☐		Learns opposites; learns sizes large and small
☐		Learns days of the week
☐		Learns patterns
☐		Actively seeks information through "why" and "how" questions
☐		Attends an activity for 10-15 minutes
☐	Personal-Social	States full name and age
☐		Engages in dramatic play, acting out full scenes
☐		Develops friendships
☐		Washes and dries hands without assistance
☐		Dresses herself
☐		Learns to handle anger
☐		Initiates play with other children and makes up games
☐		Learns manners

NOTE: All children develop at different rates. The above milestones are general guidelines for children's development. Some children are advanced in specific areas and behind in others. Consult your child's Pediatrician if there are questions or concerns.

CreativCare Learning Guides

This page is intentionally left blank

CreativCare Montessori Based Learning Guide

Ages: 3-5 Years

Cognitive Skills

Activity: Question Time

Goal: Cognitive and Expressive Language Enhancement

Supplies:

- ✓ Child's small table and chairs

Implementation:

At the latter end of this age group, the child should be able to respond to simple logic questions. The child in this age group will drive you crazy asking questions, but this is how he is starting to figure out the world.

All during the day, ask the child questions.

Ask the child to join you at the table and have a seat.

Sit down and just chat with the child.

Allow him time to talk about whatever he would like.

Afterward, try asking these logic questions:

How do we use a cup?

What do we use to brush our teeth?

Why do we use scissors?

If we pour our water out of the cup, what will happen?

What color is a lemon?

What color means hot?

What color are the leaves of a tree?

When we are hungry we need to _____?

When we are tired we need to _____?

Continue the process of asking the child questions during all activities. This enhances her cognitive skills.

Cognitive Skills

Activity: Puzzle Time

Goal: Cognitive Enhancement

Supplies:

- ✓ Child's small table and chairs
- ✓ Learning Basket
- ✓ Puzzles 12-30 pieces (3 years 5 to 10 pieces; 4 and a half to 5 up to 30 pieces)

Implementation:

Ask the child to join you at the table and have a seat.

In the Learning Basket, have at least 3 puzzles.

Tell the child you will be working with puzzles and trying to figure out where all the pieces go.

Ask the child to explore the puzzles in the Learning Basket and then choose one to work with first.

Suggest that the child take the puzzle and turn it upside down, then turn all of the pieces right side up.

Allow the child to work on the puzzle independently.

If the child is struggling, ask if you may assist.

Talk with the child about how you are looking at the pictures and matching the shapes and colors.

Teach the child about edges and matching.

Continue working on the puzzle and if the child completes the puzzle, ask if he would like to work on the next puzzle.

Before dumping the puzzle, talk about the colors and what the puzzle makes when completed.

Continue this process and always have at least 4-5 different types of puzzles.

There are puzzle books that have the actual picture and you match the pieces over the picture; these may prove easier for beginners.

There are wooden puzzles that have no particular shapes to assist, only the blank wood.

There are your jigsaw-looking puzzles with the large pieces that have the shapes of the puzzle.

Puzzles are a wonderful problem-solving activity.

CreativCare Learning Guides

Cognitive Skills

Activity: Opposites Attract

Goal: Cognitive and Fine Motor Enhancement

Supplies:

- ✓ Child's small table and chairs
- ✓ Learning Basket
- ✓ 5 pictures that you have gotten from coloring books and 5 pictures showing the opposite of the original 5 pictures (Pictures across from one another)
- ✓ Pencil

Implementation:

Ask the child to join you at the table and have a seat.

In the Learning Basket have all of the supplies listed above.

Tell the child you are going to learn about opposites.

Discuss the concepts and definitions of opposites giving examples: day and night, open and close, etc.; Opposites are two items that are different.

Instruct the child that you are going to hand her a piece of paper that has 10 pictures, 5 on one side of the page and 5 pictures across from the original 5 pictures.

Tell the child to draw a line from the picture on the left (green, remember code colors to assist with L and R memory) to the picture that is the opposite on the right (red).

Examples of pictures to use left/right side of the page:

Child smiling/Child frowning
Sunshine/Moon
Stop/Go
Front/Back
Inside/Outside
Up/Down
Snow/Flowers and Sun

Go through all of the pictures on the left and discuss what the pictures depict.

If the child is having difficulty, ask if you may assist.

Work with the child to discuss the first picture. (Example: "The little girl is smiling in this picture; what would be the opposite? How about the moon? How about a little girl frowning?")

Continue to work with the child as needed, but let her be as independent as she possibly can.

Point out opposites on a daily basis.

Cognitive Skills

Activity: Days of Week, Months, Seasons, Holidays

Goal: Cognitive and Personal Social Enhancement

Supplies:

- ✓ Chart that shows days of the week, months of the year and holidays (this can be bought or made)
- ✓ Music with songs for items listed under Activity

Implementation:

Note: There are activities that come with all charts and music, or you can create the charts and find the CD. The activities listed below are emerging activities.

Ask the child to join you on the floor each day.

Discuss what day today is and what day tomorrow will be.

Review the days of the week; sing the "today is (insert day of week)" song.

Discuss the month and describe the weather and any holidays for that month.

Review the months of the year; sing the month song.

Discuss the season and describe everything about the season.

Review the seasons; sing the season song.

Discuss holidays and describe which holiday will be coming next.

Review all of the holidays; sing the holiday song.

If these activities are reviewed on a daily basis, the child should learn the days of the week, month of the year and holidays.

Continue to review on a daily basis; add other relevant topics as indicated to the morning routine.

Cognitive Skills

Activity: Patterns All Around

Goal: Cognitive Enhancement

Supplies:

- ✓ Child's small table and chairs
- ✓ Learning Basket
- ✓ Pencil
- ✓ Draw or obtain drawings for 9 animals or objects; place the animals or objects in a line, creating a pattern; to the right of the line, place pictures of the 3 animals that will complete the pattern

Implementation:

Example of pattern:

Row 1: picture of a puppy, picture of a puppy, picture of a kitten picture of a bear

Row 2: picture of a bear, picture of a turtle, picture of a turtle, picture of a kitten

Row 3: picture of a horse, picture of a chick, picture of a horse, picture of a chick

Ask the child to join you at the table and have a seat.

In the Learning Basket are all the supplies from above.

Tell the child you will be learning about patterns; patterns define a certain series of objects or events.

Example: picture of a dog, picture of a cat, picture of a dog, the next in the series would be picture of a cat (The pattern is dog, cat, dog, cat, dog, cat.)

Tell the child he will get a worksheet with patterns and he will draw a line to the correct picture for that pattern.

Demonstrate for the child by completing the first pattern with the child.

Next, allow the child to work independently.

If the child is having difficulty, ask if you may assist and give the child clues.

Do not allow the child to get frustrated, simply work on the activity another day if needed.

Continue working on patterns and developing more sophisticated patterns for the child to explore.

Cognitive Skills Game

Activity: Size and Color Management

Goal: Cognitive and Expressive Language Enhancement

Supplies:

- ✓ Child's small table and chairs
- ✓ Learning Basket
- ✓ Objects of different sizes (large cup, small cup)
- ✓ Draw - or obtain from a coloring book - pictures of items that are different sizes (objects should be the same). Additionally, create or obtain pictures of objects that should be certain colors.
- ✓ Pencil and crayons

Implementation:

Ask the child to join you at the table and have a seat.

The Learning Basket should contain all the supplies listed above.

Start by showing the child the objects of different sizes; ask the child to identify which object is small and which object is large.

Try to have at least 3 sets of objects for the child to view.

Tell the child you have been talking about size and now you will color the object that is the smallest or largest, depending on the direction given.

Example: "Let's look at the first picture together; it asks us to find the smallest object. Color the puppy that is the smallest."
Tell the child to look at the picture carefully.

Allow the child to continue working independently and ask if you may assist if needed.

The next worksheet should have pictures of things that are always the same color, such as grass, lemon, sun, carrot, pickle, etc.

Ask the child to color the pictures the correct color of the object.

Continue working on these concepts using different methods, including everyday activities and descriptions.

Cognitive Skills Game

Activity: Maze

Goal: Cognitive Enhancement

Supplies:

- ✓ Child's small table and chairs
- ✓ Learning Basket
- ✓ Pencil
- ✓ Maze (create or obtain a maze to teach different concepts such as numbers and letters)

Example: Draw a maze that you determine the first path through what letter the object begins with. For instance, a picture of an apple and the path can go to p or you can take the a path a (take a); next path could be two cats and the path can go to the number 3 or 2 (take 2 for 2 cats).

Implementation:

Ask the child to join you at the table and have a seat.

Tell the child you will be playing a game to review the sounds the first letter in a word begins with and will review numbers through counting.

Present the maze and ask the child to grab a pencil.
Demonstrate how to choose the first path.

If needed, assist the child by working through the logic to choose paths.

For example, the next path choice might be size and which picture is larger. Ask the child to look at the two pictures and determine which is larger; the child chooses, so that is the path he will take.

Using a maze with different concepts will probably be too difficult at first, so only use sounds, size or numbers and then you can develop a more complicated maze with different concepts.

Continue challenging the child's mind on a daily basis.

Cognitive Skills Game

Activity: Board Games

Goal: Cognitive Enhancement

Supplies:

- ✓ Child's small table and chairs
- ✓ Learning Basket
- ✓ Board games such as Candy Land and Chutes and Ladders

Implementation:

Children of this age are ready to play board games, and the first board games for children are still old favorites such as Candy Land and Chutes and Ladders.

These games teach colors, numbers, counting, cooperation, taking turns and begin to teach winning and losing in life.

The games also provide invaluable quality time with your child.

Ask the child to join you on the floor; make sure all other toys are removed from the room, if possible, to minimize distractions.

Bring the game over in the Learning Basket.

Tell the child that it is game time and you will be playing Candy Land.

Explain to the child how games work, including the following:

Rules, taking turns, winners and losers.

Talk to the child about how the game works, including using colors.

Let the child choose his pawn first.

Also, let the child go first, but explain to him that sometimes you get to go second and not first.

Play the game with the child, knowing that during the first few tries, you will not get very far in the game.

Every step you get to is one step closer to teaching the child how games work, as well as reinforcing previously learned concepts of colors and numbers.

Continue to work with one game until the child is comfortable and then you can start with another game such as Chutes and Ladders.

Fine Motor Skills

Activity: Drawing Time

Goal: Fine Motor and Creativity Enhancement

Supplies:

- ✓ Learning Basket
- ✓ Crayons
- ✓ Pencil
- ✓ Markers
- ✓ Drawing paper
- ✓ Child's small table and chairs

Implementation:

At this age, a child should have good control of a pencil and crayon and should be able to copy a circle, a plus sign, and a V. Another item that should fall as a check mark on the list is drawing a house.

Ask the child to join you at the table and have a seat.

In the Learning Basket, have all of the items listed above.

Tell the child that you will be drawing and decorating your drawings.

Start the process by drawing a circle on the paper.

Ask the child to pick up the pencil and draw another circle beside your circle.

If the child has difficulty, ask if you may assist and draw another circle for her.

If there is still difficulty, try starting with the child tracing around the original circle.

Continue the same process with the plus sign and the V.

Afterward, tell the child that the next activity will be drawing a house.

The child is allowed to draw any type of house he would like.

Walk away and allow the child to have time to think about what house he would like to draw.

If the child does not begin, ask if you may assist and start to talk with him about what shape a house might look like and how to begin.

Talk with her about coloring and designing the house any way that the child chooses.

Practice drawing skills at least 3 days a week.

Fine Motor Skills

Activity: Popsicle Art

Goal: Fine Motor, Language and Cognitive Enhancement

Supplies:

- ✓ Learning Basket
- ✓ A box of popsicle sticks
- ✓ Child's small table and chairs
- ✓ Paper
- ✓ Pencil

Implementation:

Ask the child to join you at the table and have a seat.

In the Learning Basket, have all supplies listed above

Tell the child you will be making shapes in a different way.

Instruct the child that you will draw a shape on a piece of paper and then the child will create the same shape on the table using popsicle sticks.

Draw a large triangle on the piece of paper.

Ask the child to name the shape; assist if the child has difficulty.

Instruct the child make a triangle with 3 popsicle sticks.

CreativCare Learning Guides

Allow the child time to work on the project independently.
If the child is confused, ask if you may assist.

Start by showing her a trick of placing the popsicle sticks directly on the shape that was drawn.

Next, ask her to try again without the tracing feature.

If this works, move on to the next shape; if not, draw the shape one more time and ask the child to try again.

If that still does not work, tell the child you will be happy to assist her and help with this project; afterward, leave this activity for another day.

Other examples of shapes: square, rectangle, hexagon, octagon

Fine Motor Skills

Activity: I Can Write

Goal: Fine Motor, Language and Cognitive Enhancement

Supplies:

- ✓ Learning Basket
- ✓ Child's small table and chairs
- ✓ Preschool writing tablet
- ✓ Pencil
- ✓ Poster board
- ✓ Magic marker
- ✓ White paper
- ✓ Traceable plastic shapes (Spiro graph or similar)

Implementation:

By 5 years of age, a child should be able to write her first name, as well as trace shapes and other objects.

Ask the child to join you at the table and have a seat.

In the Learning Basket, have all of the supplies listed above.

Tell the child she will be writing her name, some letters and doing other fun things.

Begin the activity by taking out the poster board and writing the letters of the child's first name, the entire time slowly writing with magic marker and spelling out her name and the sounds.

Ask the child to get a white piece of paper and place over the name you have written.

Tell the child to trace the letters.

After the child traces the letters a few times, see if the child can write her name, without tracing.

If not, ask if you may assist and go back to tracing if needed.

After the child is proficient at writing her name, have her use the writing tablet to write her name.

Next, use the writing table to practice writing ABCs and 123s on a regular basis.

An emerging activity would be to practice tracing around plastic shapes or other objects. One of the best ways to work with this activity is by using Spiro graph shapes or something similar. This way, the child is tracing in different directions and will also be able to use the holes inside the shape to make different directions and pictures.

Always have the child write her name on her work.

Fine Motor Skills

Activity: Beads, Lace, and Pegs

Goal: Fine Motor, Language and Cognitive Enhancement

Supplies:

- ✓ Learning Basket
- ✓ Child's small table and chairs
- ✓ Peg board and colored pegs
- ✓ Beads to string
- ✓ Cards to lace the edges

Implementation:

Ask the child to join you at the table and have a seat.

In the Learning Basket, you will have a peg board with pegs, small beads and a small shoestring, as well as cards (animals, etc.) that have holes for the string to be laced throughout.

Tell the child you will be using our hands to work with beads, lace an animal card and play with a peg board.

Allow the child to choose which activity he would like to work with first.

For the pegs, place the board in front of the child and leave the pegs in the Learning Basket.

Instruct the child to place pegs in all of the holes, and with each peg he chooses, state the color.

Afterward, ask him to continue to layer the pegs (stack) until all of the pegs have been used.

Next, ask him to take one of the pegs and stack as many as possible on top of that one peg.

For the lace shapes, demonstrate how you hold the lace with one finger, while pulling the lace over that finger to secure the lace; if the lace is not secure the string will release.

Secure the lace and then continue to place the lace through the additional holes to outline the animal.

Allow the child to try independently before assisting.

For the beads, do not use the larger beads because these should be for younger children; get small beads with medium holes (wood beads work best) and a narrow, small shoestring.

Instruct the child to make a necklace or bracelet.

Assist if the child is having difficulty.

CreativCare Learning Guides

Fine Motor Skills

Activity: Cutting and Tracing

Goal: Fine Motor, Language and Cognitive Enhancement

Supplies:

- ✓ Learning Basket
- ✓ Child's small table and chairs
- ✓ Child's scissors
- ✓ Coloring book pictures or drawings for cutting
- ✓ White paper
- ✓ Pencil
- ✓ Crayons and/or markers

Implementation:

Ask the child to join you at the table and have a seat.

In the Learning Basket, have all the items listed above.

Tell the child you will be working with scissors, cutting and tracing.

You will also be talking about left and right today.

Begin by letting the child place whichever hand he does not write with on the piece of paper and trace his hand.

Label the hand Right or Left as indicated and have the child color the left hand green and the right hand red.

Use the green and red labels to provide clues when right and left are in question for the child.

Tell the child that the left hand is always green and the right hand is always red.

You trace the opposite hand for the child and let her color and label the appropriate name.

Depending on the skill of the child, let her trace her hand again and try to cut out her hand; if the hand is too skinny or looks too difficult, move on to cutting the picture yourself.

Demonstrate for the child how to cut out the coloring book picture.

Next, ask the child to choose a picture in the coloring book that he would like to cut; ask the child to color the picture first and then cut out the picture.

Practice for cutting, tracing and drawing is imperative at this age; it can assist in perfecting fine motor skills.

CreativCare Learning Guides

Fine Motor Skills Game

Activity: Paint Me

Goal: Fine Motor and Creativity and Imagination Enhancement

Supplies:

- ✓ Learning Basket
- ✓ Different colors of child-friendly paint
- ✓ Paint smock
- ✓ Old clothes
- ✓ Paint brushes (fine)
- ✓ Paint bucket or tray
- ✓ Outside (or gather shower curtain liners and place on the floor; you can also use an easel)

Implementation:

Tell the child to join you at the center of the room.

Advise the child you will be painting, so she will need to put on her smock.

Ask the child to pick out the brush and color she would like to use.

Tell the child she will have time to draw exactly what she desires, but first you would like for her to draw a stick figure with at least six body parts.

Make sure the child has the tools required and leave her to get started independently.

If the child is struggling with the stick figure, ask if you may assist.

Assist in getting the paint she desires into the paint tray or bucket.

Observe how the child holds the paint brush and makes specific strokes with the paint brush.

If the child seems to struggle, ask if you may assist and place your hand on top of the child's hand and the brush to assist.

Next, ask the child to name the body parts she has drawn.

Finally, this is free expression art time, so let her draw anything her heart desires and let her get messy; everything washes.

This is also a great forum to practice writing her name, numbers and letters.

Fine Motor Skills Game

Activity: Preschool Tablet

Goal: Fine Motor, Language and Cognitive Enhancement

Supplies:

- ✓ Learning Basket
- ✓ Child's small table and chairs
- ✓ Preschool electronic tablet

Implementation:

In this day and age of electronics, a preschool child needs to have a certain amount of technology throughout their day to be ready for school.

One way to accomplish this is by getting the child her own preschool electronic tablet such as the Leap Frog Leap Pad or the VTECH Innotab. There are also applications on the I pad.

This activity should be completed at least 2 days a week but should not be used to excess.

The preschool tablets have many things to offer, including downloadable games, e-reader and art functions.

Tell the child you will be working with your electronic tablet.

Allow the child to use the stylus, as well as her finger.

Working with the small stylus, as well as using fingers, will be excellent fine motor practice.

Start by reading one of the stories and allowing the child to turn the page using her finger; please note that the way we teach the Montessori style left to right will be an exception for the reading portion of this tablet; the tablet pages move from right to left

If needed, assist the child with turning the pages by moving her finger; use landmarks such as "we turn the page toward the camera."

Continue the tablet learning with using the games portion; the child must take her fingers through the maze or tap specific icons to make the game function properly.

Finally, one of the best features for fine motor skills is the artist section.

Ask the child to draw, color and create using all of her skills. She can add colors, paint, etc.

While use of this tablet should not be to excess, a child should be introduced to some type of technology at this age. A laptop or desktop computer can also be used.

Fine Motor Skills Game

Activity: Picture Perfect

Goal: Fine Motor, Language and Cognitive Enhancement

Supplies:

- ✓ Learning Basket
- ✓ Child's small table and chairs
- ✓ White paper
- ✓ Child's glue
- ✓ Crayons
- ✓ Pencil
- ✓ Scissors
- ✓ Drawing of a person and, to her right, a collage with 4 squares; each square has the letter S
- ✓ Drawing of 5 different items at the bottom, with 4 beginning with S

Implementation:

Preparation: Have a drawing of the person and collage with the 4 squares, as well as drawing of the 5 different items beginning with S (you may use pre-drawn items from coloring books or activity books).

Ask the child to join you at the table and have a seat.

In the Learning Basket, have all of the items listed above.

Tell the child you are going to play a matching, letter, cutting and drawing game.

Show the child the drawing with the collage and tell her you will use the 4 pictures to paste into this collage.

Begin working with the letter S; in these 5 pictures, there are four that begin with the letter S.

Choose the 4 pictures and color them.

If the child chooses the wrong pictures; just smile and then say "let's talk about what the pictures are and sound out the words with emphasis on the S sound."

Let the child cut out the pictures and glue them to the collage squares.

Talk about the pictures and their sounds.

You may choose whatever pictures you would like to draw or copy, and you can practice this with other letters.

All of the activities incorporate fine motor skills.

Gross Motor Skills

Activity: Move with Me

Goal: Gross Motor Enhancement

Supplies:

- ✓ Outside or large recreational room, gym
- ✓ Tumbling mats
- ✓ Good music for movement

Implementation:

Ask the child to join you outside or in the other locations noted above.

Tell her you will be practicing different types of movement.

Talk about the types of activities that have movement - playground, dance, running, etc.

Talk about bending, twisting, stretching, and galloping.

Tell the child that you will be playing music to do these activities.

Make sure there is plenty of space for these activities.

Start with a slow song and show the child how to stretch with arms to the side and slowly move them upward and back down again; you can show her to take a breath in and out, but that will probably be difficult for this age group.

CreativCare Learning Guides

Note: Begin all activities slowly and speed up as you go along.

Next, show the child how to bend at the waist half way down.

Child repeats.

Next, show the child how to bend at the waist all the way down and touch her toes without bending her knees.

Child repeats.

Next, show the child how to twist slowly side to side, back and forth.

Child repeats.

Next, speed things up a bit and show the child how to skip around the room.

Child repeats.

Show the child how to gallop around the room.

Child repeats.

If the child has difficulty with any of the tasks, make sure to take the time to demonstrate again and assist as needed.

Move on and come back to a task another day if needed.

With all of the tasks after the slow version, speed up the music and the task.

Another great motion to practice with preschoolers is how to freeze/stand still.

This is an excellent way to get the child to stop if she is running away from you or close to danger and you cannot reach her in time; simply teach her to freeze.

Gross Motor Skills

Activity: Fantastic Gymnastics

Goal: Gross Motor Enhancement

Supplies:

- ✓ Outside or large recreational room, gym
- ✓ Tumbling mats
- ✓ Balance beam
- ✓ Yarn or tape

Implementation:

Ask the child to join you outside or in the other locations noted above.

Tell her you will be learning and working on gymnastic exercises.

One of the first things to learn is balance and control.

Ask the child to stand on one foot and balance (stay close so he does not fall); the child should have this ability for at least 3 seconds.

If the child is unsure or can't perform the activity, demonstrate and have the child try again; if he still has difficulty, move on to the next activity for now.
Next, take a piece of yarn or colored duct tape (ask the parent what he prefers) 2-3 feet long and place it in the center of the room.

Ask the child to balance and walk along the line; demonstrate this task as it is more difficult. Demonstrate walking forward and walking back to the original location.

Let the child try but do not let her get frustrated; it is best to move to another activity and come back to this one later if the child is frustrated.

The next activity will be forward rolling.

Demonstrate on the mat how to roll forward, watching the child's neck during this process.

The next activity will be trying a hand stand; if you are unable to perform this maneuver, show the child with a doll or on a video.

While the child is learning, you should be holding her steady and upright.

All of these skills are great for gross motor development.

CreativCare Learning Guides

Gross Motor Skills

Activity: Trikes and Bikes

Goal: Gross Motor Enhancement

Supplies:

- ✓ Outside or at a park or empty parking lot
- ✓ Tricycle and Bicycle

Implementation:

At 3-4 years of age, the child should have a tricycle or similar ride-on vehicle. By 4-5 years of age, the child should have a bicycle with training wheels. By 5 years of age, the training wheels should be starting to come off.

Bikes and tricycles are excellent gross motor toys that allow physical exercise, as well as hours of fun and exploration.

Note: Always, even with a tricycle, make sure the child has a safety approved helmet; knee pads and elbow pads are optional but a good idea.

Start by working with the 3 year old daily, if possible, using the tricycle, learning to steer and pedal.

Note: There are tricycles available that allow the parent to steer until the child is old enough to reach the pedals; at that time, the parent steering bar is removed.

Describe all the things that the child sees while on the tricycle.

The child should have good balance skills when he moves to the bicycle with training wheels.

This allows the child to have her independence, while learning to ride a bike.

When the child is ready, remove the training wheels and start by standing beside the child, holding onto the bike.

Continue this process until the child shows signs of readiness for you to let go.

Make sure that the child is learning and riding in a safe environment.

Gross Motor Skills

Activity: Balls in the Air and Everywhere

Goal: Gross Motor Enhancement

Supplies:

- ✓ Outside or at a park or empty parking lot
- ✓ Ball - Nerf or plastic
- ✓ Basketball
- ✓ Nerf Football

Implementation:

Gross motor skills also require being able to manage and catch balls. This should be an introduction time to different sports and balls.

Tell the child you are going to work on catching and throwing balls.

Hand the child the Nerf ball and have her throw the ball to you.

Notice how the child throws and if it is underhanded, work with her on other types of throws, such as overhanded.

Throw the ball to the child and see if she is able to catch.

If not, go back to basics and teach the child how to catch the ball by cupping her hands.

Teach the child to always keep her eye on the ball.
Work on this task and move on to other balls, such as the basketball.

One way to start teaching this is with small basketball hoops and sets.

Work on dribbling the basketball.

Demonstrate how to dribble the ball, bouncing it up and down against your hand.

Allow the child to practice this technique.

Next, teach the child about football by starting with a Nerf football.

Show the child the proper way to hold the football and catch.

Continue all processes above until the child is comfortable playing with all the above types of balls, including throwing, dribbling and catching.

Do not allow the child to become frustrated; there is always tomorrow to work with the different types of balls.

Gross Motor Skills

Activity: March to the Beat

Goal: Gross Motor Enhancement

Supplies:

- ✓ Marching music
- ✓ Ample space to move and jump

Implementation:

Tell the child you are going to learn about marching, jumping and acting like a sea creature.

Start by demonstrating how to march in place; talk about who marches and that you march in groups mainly.

Ask the child to follow you and march around the room, emphasizing picking up your feet to the beat.

Next, tell the child to jump, jump, jump, like a kangaroo.

If he has difficulty, assist with a demonstration of how to jump.

Practice jumping like a kangaroo and then long jumping.

Finally, demonstrate for the child how to walk like a crab (all fours with your legs spread out).

Let the child walk like a crab with you.

Review what you have learned and ask the child to march; do not demonstrate unless the child is confused.

Ask the child to jump like a kangaroo and then complete a long jump.

Ask the child to walk like a crab.

Use the remainder of the time for this activity to ask the child to imitate the motions of a favorite animal.

Offer suggestions of monkey, rabbit, etc., as needed.

Gross Motor Skills Game

Activity: It's a Ballgame

Goal: Gross Motor Enhancement

Supplies:

- ✓ Outside or at a park
- ✓ Child's plastic bat and ball
- ✓ Optional: Toy automatic ball thrower
- ✓ Optional: Ball tee

Implementation:

You have already worked on catching a ball, so now we move on to playing ball by teaching hitting and running.

Tell the child you will be playing ball; we will hit, catch and run.

Explain the rules of the game to the child; the first step is practicing catching and then learning to hit.

Show the child the correct way to hold a bat (hands together and holding the bat back.

Start with the ball sitting on the tee, if available, and let him practice swinging to hit the ball.

Place your hands over the child's hands and show him how to swing.

Practice swinging before the ball is actually pitched.

Continue this process throughout the week, advancing to actually throwing the ball or using a thrower in the weeks to come.

Move forward to teaching the child to catch the ball in the outfield.

Next, show him how to hit and run around the bases.

This is a process that will take several weeks, but the child will be very proud when he learns to play.

This activity demonstrates multiple aspects of the gross motor skills needed for this age.

CreativCare Learning Guides

Gross Motor Skills Game

Activity: I've Got Rhythm

Goal: Gross Motor Enhancement

Supplies:

- ✓ Music
- ✓ Ample space
- ✓ Two chairs and a broom stick

Implementation:

One of the easiest ways to work on gross motor skills is through dance. There are all kinds of dances and movements, and each movement creates excellent exercise.

Start by telling the child you are going to have dance time and do some special things while you dance.

The first dance is called the limbo.

Set up two tall chairs and place a broom stick over the two chairs.

Demonstrate for the child how to limbo by bending at the back and going under the stick, without touching the stick.

Allow the child to try; if he fails, just smile and say, "Let's try again; this can be very tricky."

Continue to work on the limbo game.

Next, play music that will allow the child to express himself, including clapping to the beat of the music.

Demonstrate how to clap with the beats if needed.

Finally, allow a time of free dance when the child can move and do anything that he pleases.

During this time, encourage different movements of bending over, reaching high, clapping, jumping and twisting.

Gross Motor Skills Game

Activity: Obstacle Course

Goal: Gross Motor Enhancement

Supplies:

- ✓ Play set or park playground
- ✓ Red ribbon
- ✓ 4-6 hula hoops
- ✓ Ball and bucket
- ✓ Jump rope

Implementation:

If you complete this activity in the back yard, have everything set up prior to beginning. If you complete the activity away from home, let the child assist in setting up everything at the park.

Tell the child you are going to work with an obstacle course.

Make sure there is a sliding board and, if possible, a rope ladder.

Place a ball on the ground; about 3-4 feet away, place a bucket.

Place 4-6 hula hoops in line side-by-side in twos.

Next, place a jump rope straight across.

Move several feet further to the nearest tree and place the red ribbon.

Take the child to each obstacle course station and show him what to do one by one:

1. Go to the rope ladder (if available) and climb into the house and down the slide, or just climb up the slide and slide down if no rope ladder is available.
2. Go to the ball, pick up the ball and try to throw the ball into the bucket or basket.
3. Step into each hula hoop left, then right, left, then right through each hoop.
4. Run to the rope and jump across or, if you can, play jump rope through 3 jumps.
5. Lastly, run and grab the red ribbon.

This course layout is merely an example; you can use whatever you have available, but make sure there are at least 5 different obstacles.

Change the course around and add new obstacles for a different game.

Language Skills

Activity: Story Time

Goal: Receptive and Expressive Language Enhancement

Supplies:

- ✓ Learning Basket
- ✓ Colored construction paper
- ✓ Hole punch
- ✓ Colored yarn (at least 3 colors)
- ✓ Child safe glue
- ✓ Children's book (length of Little Golden Books)
- ✓ Child's small table and chairs
- ✓ 15-20 cutout pictures that the child is not familiar with or has seen very few times

Implementation:

Preparation: Cut out 15-20 pictures of things that the child has very little exposure to or has seen only a few times.

At this age, a child should be able to pay attention to a 10-15 minute story.

Tell the child to join you at the table and have a seat.

In the Learning Basket, have all of the materials listed above.

Tell the child that the first activity of your time today will be reading the story of *Doc Mcstuffins Goes to the Zoo*. Remember the book should last for about 10-15 minutes.

Ask the child to put on her listening ears and help read the story.

During the story, make sure to describe all of the pictures and activities in the book, as well as ask the child questions of what is happening in the book.

It is an emerging skill, but some children are able to read a few words at this age.

Next, tell the child there is another activity; you will be making a scrap book.

Ask the child to look at the pictures and choose 10 pictures.

Give the child time to choose the pictures.

After the child has chosen the pictures, let the child pick out the colors of construction paper that he prefers.

Next, let him pick out the colors of yarn he prefers to tie the book together.

Throughout each step, describe to the child what he is doing and why he is doing it.

Depending on the amount of time and the child's attention span, you might need to end the activity here and complete the book the next day.

The remainder of the activity is as follows:

Ask the child to apply the child safe glue to the construction paper or the back of the picture.

Paste the picture in the book.

Before moving to the next picture, make sure that you describe all aspects of the picture - color, size, shape, etc.
Then, allow the child to move on to the next picture.

Continue this process until all pictures are pasted in the book.

Make it a habit to review this book regularly.

After the child learns all aspects of the 10 pictures, add new pictures to the book and begin the process again.

Language Skills

Activity: Name and Color Recognition

Goal: Expressive and Receptive Language Enhancement

Supplies:

- ✓ Learning Basket
- ✓ Coloring book pictures or drawings of an item that has 12 different spaces with 6 of the spaces blank and the other six with the words
- ✓ Yellow, red and blue crayons
- ✓ 4 pictures of animals or objects that are to be the color yellow
- ✓ A trace section of the word yellow beside each animal or object
- ✓ A read section by each animal or object saying "your"

Implementation:

Note: This activity is an emerging skill for a 4 and a half to 5 year old child.

Preparation:

A coloring book picture or drawing of an object that has 12 different spaces with 6 of the spaces blank and the other six with the words yellow, red and blue

Example: Coloring book picture or drawing of twelve balloons with every other balloon stating the word yellow, red or blue; the other six balloons will have no words.

A page with 3 categories: READ, TRACE, COLOR.

Example: Under the Read category, it will say "your"; under the Trace category, it will have the word "yellow" in traceable letters; under the color category, it will have a picture to be colored or an animal or object that is always yellow, such as a lemon.

READ	TRACE	COLOR
Your	Yellow (Broken lines for learning to write)	picture of sun

Complete four of the above categories.

Tell the child to join you at the table and have a seat.

Bring over the Learning Basket with all supplies.

Tell the child you will be learning about the color yellow.

Discuss several items that are colored yellow.

Discuss how to phonetically say the word "yellow" and how it is spelled.

Show the child in writing how the word "yellow" looks and is spelled.

Ask the child to take the yellow crayon and color the balloons that say yellow.

Talk briefly about the other colors and her words.

If the child colors the incorrect balloon, just smile and say, "Let's talk about the word 'yellow'; 'yellow' begins with a Y." Assist the child as needed to find the correct balloons.

CreativCare Learning Guides

Next, show the child the other activity of Read, Trace and Color.

First, read everything saying, "Your Yellow Sun," etc.

Point with your finger after each word.

Next, show the child how to trace the word "yellow."

Finally, allow the child to color the picture of the object beside the trace section.

Continue this process with all major colors .

Language Skills

Activity: 1, 2, 3

Goal: Expressive and Receptive Language Enhancement

Supplies:

- ✓ Preschool writing tablet
- ✓ Pencil
- ✓ Foam or plastic numbers (magnetic numbers would be best)

Implementation:

At this age, the child should continue working on number concepts. There are many activities to work on these concepts, but one of the best is simply count all day long whenever you have a chance during the child's daily routine.

Examples:

Stairs: If the house has stairs, count each stair as you go up and down.

Blocks: Count the number of blocks the child is using to build something; count them as he tries to build, and when the house or tower is done, count the total number of blocks again.

Books: If the child has a bookshelf or place books are stored, count the number of books.

Snacks: Count the number of crackers or cookies in a bowl; count the number again as the child eats the crackers.

CreativCare Learning Guides

Meals: Count the number of items on the child's plate; count the number of eggs in a carton.

Letters: Count the number of letters or pieces of mail that arrive each day.

Everything that you can do to involve counting, including the number of footsteps it takes to get to the bathroom, will help develop the child's counting skills.

Start working with the child on numbers and what they look like.

Use the foam or magnetic numbers to have a "number of the day."

Have the child copy the number of the day on the preschool paper.

Additionally, the child should be able to count to 20 at this point.

Language Skills

Activity: My Information

Goal: Expressive and Receptive Language Enhancement

Supplies:

- ✓ Book about a character that moves to a new home
- ✓ Rocking chair or couch

Implementation:

Tell the child to join you in the rocking chair or on the couch.

Ask the child, "What is your name?" The child should know his first and last name.

Ask the child, "How old are you?" The child should know his age but may use fingers to show you.

Ask the child, "When is your birthday?" Work with the child if he does not know.

Read the child a story about a character that moves to a new home.

Talk to the child about the character that is moving.

Describe to the child that the character is moving to a new address.

Tell the child that everyone has an address; an address is the location where you live.

Tell the child that you will be working on learning the child's address. Start by breaking down the address for easier learning.

1234 Japan Lane
Raleigh, NC 27606

Start by working on the 1234; "You live at 1234." Show the child the numbers in writing.

After the child learns 1234, move on to Japan Lane.

Continue this process until the child knows his address.

It is imperative that a child know his full name and address in case he is ever lost.

Language Skills

Activity: ABCs and Phonics Fun

Goal: Expressive and Receptive Language Enhancement

Supplies:

- ✓ VTECH ABC *Refrigerator Magnet* or similar product
- ✓ Preschool/Kindergarten writing tablet
- ✓ Pencil
- ✓ Coloring book pictures or drawings of an animal or object that begins with a specific letter; beside that drawing, have four other drawings - one of the drawings beginning with the same letter but the other three not beginning with the same letter
- ✓ Child's small table and chairs
- ✓ Learning Basket

Implementation:

Preparation: Have the ABC Refrigerator Magnet game on the refrigerator; make the coloring book pictures or drawn pictures as indicated below:

Example:

Picture of a cat: In the row beside the cat, draw a picture or get a picture of a cup, dog, plate and flower.

The child will be asked to color the picture that begins with the same letter as "cat."

CreativCare Learning Guides

Ask the child to join you at the refrigerator. Each day, have a letter of the day; the VTECH unit will say the letter and all sounds that the letter makes.

Ask the child to repeat the sounds the letter of the day makes.

Next, ask the child to join you at the table and have a seat.

In the Learning Basket, have all of the above listed items with the exception of the refrigerator magnet game.

Tell the child you will be learning about the letter _____. Ask the child to tell you the letter based on the refrigerator game you just played.

Assist the child as needed.

Example:

Give the child the writing tablet and let him trace the letter C; ask the child what sounds the letter C makes.

Afterward, tell the child you are going to be working more with the letter C.

Show the child your drawing and ask him what is the picture located on the left.

The child should say "cat"; ask him what the word "cat" starts with and make the sound.

Instruct the child to review the additional pictures located on the right and color the picture that starts with a C just like "cat."

Continue this process on a regular basis using the same format and all of letters of the alphabet

CreativCare Learning Guides

Language Skills Game

Activity: Story-telling Puppet

Goal: Expressive and Receptive Language, Creativity

Supplies:

- ✓ Learning Basket
- ✓ Sock or brown paper lunch bag
- ✓ Yarn, buttons, crayons, markers
- ✓ Child safe glue
- ✓ Child's small table and chairs

Implementation:

Ask the child to join you at the table and have a seat.

In the Learning Basket, place all of the supplies in the above list.

Tell the child you will be making puppets and tomorrow, you will be acting out a story.

Ask the child to choose a sock or bag to make her puppet; you will make a puppet too.

Request that the child choose the items to decorate her puppet.

The child should use yarn for hair; crayons, markers or buttons for the mouth, etc.

Allow the child plenty of time to decorate her puppet.

Tell the child you will decorate the puppet and let it dry overnight.

The next day, ask the child to join you at the table again and have her puppet and yours in the Learning Basket.

Tell the child you are going to have a puppet show about anything the child desires, as long as the show is talking about the past and the future.

Discuss what the past and the future means and, if needed, assist the child with making his play.

Example: "Yesterday, we went to the park and saw birds and we played on the slide and in the sand; tomorrow we will be going to the children's museum to look at animals."

Allow the child to make up any story that she would like.

Language Skills Game

Activity: Word Find

Goal: Expressive and Receptive Language and Cognitive

Supplies:

- ✓ Child's small table and chairs
- ✓ Poster board
- ✓ Blue or black marker

Implementation:

Preparation: Looking around the room, write down 15-20 items; take those items and make small cards with the name of the word on the poster board written in blue or black marker.

Example:

Pillow, chair, lamp, table, rug, etc.

Beside or underneath the objects that you have written, place the cards face down.

Ask the child to join you at the table and have a seat.

Tell him you are going to have fun with words and objects.

Explain that there are cards hidden around the room under some objects.

The child is to pick up the card and try to sound out the word.

Afterward, you will ask, "What is the object?"

Example:

The child finds a card under the blue pillow.
The child picks up the card and sounds out Piiiii lo lo lo.
When asked what the item is, the child says "pillow."
You will state, using the phonics, "pillow" and spell "pillow."

Move to the next word.

This is a game that you can play many times as you change the cards.

Language Skills Game

Activity: Connect the Dots

Goal: Expressive and Receptive Language and Cognitive

Supplies:

- ✓ Child's small table and chairs
- ✓ Drawing for Connect the Dots using the alphabet
- ✓ Pencil
- ✓ Learning Basket

Implementation:

Preparation: Draw or trace a coloring book picture of anything. If you trace the picture, add dots and erase the lines in between the dots; if you draw the picture, simply draw with dots.

Ask the child to join you at the table and have a seat.

Tell him you are going to talk about sequence and the alphabet.

Ask the child to say the entire alphabet.

Afterward, tell him you are going to play a game with the alphabet and to find each letter in order. Example: A, then B, then C, etc.

Tell the child to find the letter A.

Afterward, tell the child to find the letter B.

Next, ask the child to take his pencil and draw a line from A to B.
If this is difficult, demonstrate for the child.

You can also complete this game using numbers.

Assist the child as needed, but always let him work independently when possible.

You could even make a dot to dot of a letter or a number.

This activity is educational and fun for the child to see what the dots will make.

CreativCare Learning Guides

Personal-Social Skills

Activity: All Dressed Now

Goal: Personal-Social Skill Enhancement

Supplies:

- ✓ None Required
- ✓ Optional: Tie shoe tool; Dress-up doll with a shoe that ties

Implementation:

By 4-5 years of age, the child should be able to primarily dress himself. The child should be able to put his clothes on and by 5 years of age, should be able to button, as well as tie shoes.

In this society, there are not as many shoes that tie because everything is made with velcro. Make a point to have at least one pair of shoes that your child needs to tie or create your own tying practice tool or use a dress up doll with shoelaces.

On a daily basis, make sure the child has the opportunity to practice getting dressed independently.

Talk with the parents and make sure the child is having this opportunity when getting dressed each day.

Tell the child you are going to practice buttoning, snapping, tying and zipping.

If the child does not have these options on his clothes, use a dress up doll. Work on one task at a time, such as beginning with zipping or snapping, which is easier.

Assist the child as needed with the task.

Most children know how to get dressed but fail to be able to button and tie.

Getting dressed without assistance is an important skill to have at 5 years old and promotes independence.

CreativCare Learning Guides

Personal-Social Skills

Activity: Anger Management

Goal: Personal-Social Skill Enhancement

Supplies:

- ✓ Learning Basket
- ✓ Puppet and puppet show on anger
- ✓ Book about dealing with anger

Implementation:

Preparation: Read a children's book about anger and how to handle anger; write or obtain a puppet show about anger.

Example: The puppet show could be about bedtime and how the child is angry because he would rather stay up and play a game than go to bed. The child becomes very angry and then sad.

The parent would explain that we know you are angry, but it is a weeknight and bedtime is now, and he can play the game first thing tomorrow.

If you would like some time by yourself for a moment, you may go to your room.

You can write any puppet show that you choose and you can use a puppet you have or a sock puppet that you create.
Ask the child to join you on the floor in the center of the room.

Tell him you are going to talk about emotions, specifically anger.

Discuss what anger is and what it looks like.

Read a book about anger and talk with the child; ask the child to tell you things that make him angry or mad.

Next, bring out the puppet and perform the show.

Discuss all of the emotions the puppet felt about his bedtime, etc.

At this age, a child should be able to handle his anger appropriately.

Personal-Social Skills

Activity: Responsibility

Goal: Personal-Social and Societal Process Emersion

Supplies:

- ✓ Learning Basket
- ✓ Children's book about responsibility
- ✓ Scenarios about responsibility

Implementation:

Ask the child to join you at the table and have a seat.

Tell the child you will be learning about responsibility and taking care of things.

Ask the child what the word "responsibility" means.

Discuss with the child the meaning of responsibility using different scenarios, such as if you take a toy with you to the mall, you are responsible; if your job is to feed the puppy, it is your responsibility, etc.

Afterward, read a book about responsibility.

Discuss all the aspects of the book and ask the child her thoughts about the book.

Next, tell the child that you are going to play a game.

Create scenarios about responsibility and ask the child questions regarding those scenarios.

Example:

Jay's mom is responsible for taking the puppy outside every morning; the puppy had an accident. Who is responsible?

Jay is responsible for taking his backpack to school and not losing his pencil; Jay left his pencil on the teacher's desk. Who is responsible?

Austin's mom is responsible for making his lunch every day. When it was time for school, Austin went to get his lunch and there was none. Who is responsible?

During the day, try to give the child some responsibility, such as cleaning up his toys.

Continue the responsibility discussion on a regular basis.

Personal-Social Skills

Activity: Manners All The Way, Every Single Day

Goal: Personal-Social Skills and Societal Requirement Enhancement

Supplies:

- ✓ Learning Basket
- ✓ Coloring pages about manners or create your own drawings about manners
- ✓ Crayons
- ✓ Scenarios about manners
- ✓ Child's small table and chairs

Implementation:

Ask the child to join you at the table and have a seat.

Tell the child you are going to discuss manners; ask the child what manners mean.

The child is likely to say, "when you say please and thank you."

Discuss with the child that manners mean how you act and behave around others. Manners encompass many aspects of life.

Discuss the following manners:
Interrupting people when they are talking or busy
Table manners
Greetings
Respect
Tact
Gossip
Being sorry

Find or create some coloring pages about manners, talking to the child about what he is coloring.

Try using some scenarios about manners and ask the child about the scenarios.

Example:

A little bear needs to speak with his mom and she is on the phone. Should the little bear:

    A. Wait until his mom is off of the phone
    B. Interrupt saying, "I want a cookie."

A turtle sees a frog first thing in the morning and he is blocking the path. What should he say?

    A. "Get out of my way."
    B. "Good Morning, could you please move over a little?"

A lion meets a zebra and notices the zebra looks different. What should he say?

    A. "Hi, I like your stripes."
    B. "You are funny looking; what is wrong with you?"

CreativCare Learning Guides

Personal-Social Skills

Activity: Germ Fighters

Goal: Fine Motor and Creativity Enhancement

Supplies:

- ✓ Learning Basket
- ✓ Kleenex
- ✓ Hand Soap, sink and water
- ✓ Pictures of proper hand-washing and germs or coloring book pictures
- ✓ Child's small table and chairs

Implementation:

Ask the child to join you at the table and have a seat.

Tell the child you will be talking about germs.

Ask the child what a germ is and where germs are found.

Discuss that germs are everywhere, and one of the most common places are people's hands.

Proper hand-washing involves warm water (when available), soap and a paper towel or towel.

Remind the child that your hands should be washed for 20 seconds or 1 round of the ABC song.

Take the child to the sink and review hand washing techniques.
Tell him that another germ-buster is using a Kleenex.

Discuss how we use a Kleenex; talk about what is and is not acceptable behavior, including picking your nose.

Continue discussing how to cover your mouth when you sneeze, including what to do if there is not Kleenex - use your hand or arm to cover your mouth and then wash hands immediately.

Show the child pictures or have him color hand washing, sneezing or germ pictures.

Personal-Social Skills Game

Activity: Magnetic Force

Goal: Personal-Social, Fine Motor and Cognitive Enhancement

Supplies:

- ✓ Child's small table and chairs
- ✓ Learning Basket
- ✓ "Melissa and Doug" magnetic/wooden dolls (There are boy versions as well.)

Implementation:

Ask the child to join you at the table and have a seat.

Tell the child that we have been discussing getting dressed, and you know how to dress yourself; now let's play a game and practice dressing a wooden doll.

Ask the child to remove the wooden doll and all clothes from the basket.

Tell the child that his first task is to separate all of the clothes (tops, bottoms, shoes).

Give the child ample time to explore and dress the doll the way she pleases.

Next, ask the child to find a shirt and place it on the doll.

Ask the child to find the pants that match in color with the shirt and place on the doll.

Afterward, ask him to find the shoes.

Playing with the wooden doll is good practice for getting dressed.

Use this time as a discussion time about dressing and how well the child is doing at dressing himself.

You can also use this time to revisit the dress-up animal or doll.

CreativCare Learning Guides

Personal-Social Skills Game

Activity: Friends and Fun

Goal: Fine Motor and Creativity Enhancement

Supplies:

- ✓ Friends
- ✓ Stuffed animals

Implementation:

It is very important that the child continues to have interaction with friends and new acquaintances. At 4 or 5 years old, the child will likely go to a preschool or Kindergarten and must know how to cooperate and share with other children.

Talk with the child before she has a friend come to play or before she meets friends at the park, etc.

Remind the child that we have to share, take turns, listen, follow the rules and cooperate.

Remind the child it is important that we are always nice to our friends.

Tell the child you will play a game to get ready to spend time with your friends.

Pretend that stuffed bears, dogs, and kittens are your friends.

"Show me how you greet your friends."

"If your friend is playing with a car that you would like, show me how you would obtain the car."

"If the rules of the game are to run in a circle and you are hopping, are you following the rules?"

Tell the child, "We are leaving now to play with your friends but after one hour, we will be leaving the park." The child should accept limits.

Continue working with the child regarding social situations and proper actions.

Review greetings and ongoing conversation with the child.

Personal-Social Skills Game

Activity: Social Situations

Goal: Personal-Social and Societal Expectations Enhancement

Supplies:

- ✓ Learning Basket
- ✓ Poster board
- ✓ Crayons and markers
- ✓ Index cards

Implementation:

Ask the child to join you at the table and have a seat.

Tell the child you are going to make your very own game about behavior and proper manners.

Give the child a choice in what type of game he would like to make: Maze, Board Game, Dot to Dot, Logic Questions.

Whichever game the child chooses, use the poster board to make the actual game and the index cards as instruction cards for how many spaces to move forward, etc.

Make the game using scenarios about social situations.

Example:

"Logan is playing tag with his friends. Logan was told not to go beyond the big tree because these were the limits set by his mom."

"Should Logan go beyond the big tree because his friend asked him to and his friend's mom said Logan could go further? If your answer is correct, move two squares closer to the Nice tree."

    A. Yes, friend's mom said Logan could go further
    B. No, Logan's mom set the limit at the big tree

"Mason is playing with a friend, and the friend has a fire truck. Mason would like to play with the fire truck."

"How should Mason obtain the fire truck? If your answer is correct, move forward 4 spaces to the Nice tree."

    A. Mason should ask nicely if he may play with the fire truck.
    B. Mason should grab the fire truck and run.

For mazes or dot to dots, you would use the scenarios as the right path to take.

Example: "Blow your nose on your sleeve" would be one path of the maze and "use a Kleenex" would be the other.

Chapter 7: Key Concepts

Throughout this book, we have provided activities for ages 3 months to 5 years, guided by Montessori principles. Additionally, we discussed the key concepts of the Montessori teaching theoretical framework.

Some of the more important key concepts of the Montessori framework are as follows: use the same work station daily, all learning tools are in a tray or basket, all learning tools are organized and accessible, never assist the child before asking, use items from the child's environment when possible, and always allow the child time to explore any activity.

In addition to the Montessori theoretical framework, there are key Child Development concepts that are an essential part of a child's successful development. These concepts involve peers, music, language and the environment.

Even though working with a caregiver on a one to one basis is an asset, it is imperative that a child receives social interaction with peers on a regular basis. Listed below are several venues that offer both peer interaction and education at the same time.

- ❖ Children's museum
- ❖ Story-time at the local library
- ❖ Gymnastics or recreation classes
- ❖ Sunday school and church groups
- ❖ Mall play areas
- ❖ Organized play dates
- ❖ Parks and play grounds
- ❖ Barnes and Noble activities
- ❖ Indoor playgrounds

Other key concepts include the importance of incorporating music, books, and outside time with every age group. Even the youngest infant will benefit from a life filled with music, books, and adventure outdoors. Use every opportunity during the day to explain and teach the child. Ensure that each day is filled with open-ended time, so the child can choose his/her own activity.

The goal should be to make every day fun and, during the daily activities, find teachable moments. Always make sure the caregiver and parent are on the same page and have the same educational goals. "The Difference is education!"

1

12-18 Months, *173, 174, 175*
18-24 Months, *252, 253, 254*

3

3-6 Months, *11, 12, 13*

6

6-12 Months, *90, 91, 92*

A

Activity, *13, 15, 17, 19, 21, 23, 25, 26, 28, 30, 32, 34, 35, 37, 39, 41, 43, 45, 47, 49, 51, 52, 54, 56, 57, 60, 62, 64, 66, 68, 70, 72, 74, 76, 78, 80, 81, 83, 85, 87, 89, 92, 94, 96, 98, 100, 102, 104, 105, 108, 109, 111, 113, 115, 117, 119, 121, 123, 125, 126, 127, 129, 131, 133, 135, 137, 139, 144, 146, 148, 150, 152, 154, 156, 158, 160, 162, 164, 166, 168, 170, 172, 175, 177, 179, 181, 183, 185, 187, 189, 190, 192, 194, 196, 198, 200, 202, 204, 206, 208, 210, 212, 214, 216, 218, 220, 222, 224, 225, 227, 229, 231, 233, 235, 237, 239, 241, 243, 245, 247, 249, 254, 257, 259, 261, 263, 265, 267, 269, 271, 273, 275, 277, 279, 281, 283, 285, 287, 289, 292, 294, 296, 298, 300, 302, 304, 306, 308, 310, 312, 314, 316, 318, 320, 322, 324, 326, 328, 330, 332, 334, 339, 341, 343, 345, 347, 349, 351, 353, 355, 357, 359, 361, 363, 365, 367, 370, 371, 373, 375, 377, 379, 381, 383, 385, 387, 389, 391, 393, 395, 397, 399, 401, 403, 405, 407, 409, 412, 414, 416, 418, 423, 425, 427, 429, 431, 433, 435, 437, 439, 441, 443, 445, 447, 449, 451, 453, 455, 457, 459, 461, 463, 465, 467, 469, 470, 474, 477, 479, 481, 482, 485, 487, 489, 491, 493, 495, 497, 499, 501, 503*
Animal, *150, 381*

B

ball, *25, 60, 98, 104, 124, 125, 128, 173, 210, 211, 245, 251, 252, 279, 281, 282, 287, 288, 292, 306, 312, 313, 371, 373, 375, 383, 389, 396, 407, 417, 420, 421, 461, 462, 465, 466, 469, 470*
block, *95, 116, 241, 242, 257, 258, 351, 352*
book, *1, 6, 9, 60, 90, 93, 102, 108, 141, 172, 181, 198, 199, 202, 203, 212, 247, 248, 261, 262, 269, 270, 271, 289, 306, 310, 311, 319, 320, 322, 332, 333, 337, 338, 359, 362, 387, 388, 392, 401, 405, 412, 413, 447, 471, 472, 473, 474, 481, 491, 492, 493, 505*

C

caregiver, *11, 15, 17, 75, 149, 164, 165, 166, 189, 225, 227, 228, 245, 345, 355, 357, 359, 368, 373, 378, 407, 505, 506*
Child Markers, *302*
Child-Sized furniture, *8*
Cognitive Skills, *7, 13, 15, 17, 19, 21, 23, 25, 26, 92, 94, 96, 98, 175, 177, 179, 181, 183, 185, 187, 189, 192, 202, 204, 254, 257, 259, 261, 263, 339, 341, 343, 345, 347, 383, 414, 423, 425, 427, 429, 431*
colored construction paper, *261, 318, 332, 339*
coloring book, *194, 200, 271, 272, 350, 355, 356, 359, 392, 433, 448, 474, 481, 487, 497*
CreativCare Services, *7, 11, 12, 90, 91, 173, 174, 252, 253, 337, 338, 421, 422*
cup, *91, 160, 161, 174, 211, 227, 229, 230, 237, 238, 241, 242, 245, 246, 253, 313,*

328, 329, 330, 336, 351, 352, 389, 390, 393, 399, 407, 408, 423, 424, 481

D

developmental checklist, 1, 7
doll, 146, 163, 206, 212, 216, 235, 290, 308, 309, 324, 325, 331, 334, 377, 397, 401, 403, 404, 416, 417, 458, 489, 499, 500
draw, 200, 271, 300, 302, 303, 314, 349, 356, 368, 420, 427, 432, 439, 440, 441, 442, 449, 450, 452, 454, 481, 487
dress, 163, 253, 324, 397, 489, 499, 500
dumping, 255, 341, 353, 426

E

Electronic tablet
  Innotab and Leap Frog, 451
emerging activity, 323, 444
environment, 9, 55, 85, 188, 405, 406, 460, 505
explore, 32, 37, 39, 40, 49, 60, 98, 104, 106, 108, 110, 111, 112, 122, 124, 188, 189, 199, 200, 209, 229, 250, 258, 259, 260, 262, 267, 268, 273, 275, 276, 280, 287, 301, 308, 319, 324, 365, 425, 499, 505

F

Fine Motor, 7, 28, 30, 32, 34, 35, 37, 39, 41, 94, 105, 106, 107, 108, 109, 110, 111, 113, 114, 115, 117, 118, 119, 120, 131, 160, 190, 192, 194, 196, 198, 200, 202, 204, 267, 271, 273, 275, 277, 279, 281, 283, 284, 285, 300, 355, 357, 359, 361, 363, 365, 367, 370, 412, 427, 439, 441, 443, 445, 447, 449, 451, 453, 497, 499, 501
folding,, 357

G

Game, 23, 25, 26, 52, 54, 56, 68, 70, 72, 83, 85, 87, 100, 102, 104, 115, 117, 119, 131, 133, 135, 150, 152, 154, 166, 168, 170, 185, 187, 189, 200, 202, 204, 216, 218, 220, 231, 233, 235, 245, 247, 249, 265, 267, 269, 281, 283, 285, 298, 300, 302, 314, 316, 318, 330, 332, 334, 349, 351, 353, 365, 367, 370, 381, 383, 385, 407, 409, 412, 414, 416, 418, 433, 435, 437, 449, 451, 453, 465, 467, 469, 482, 484, 487, 499, 501, 503
Goal, 13, 15, 17, 19, 21, 23, 25, 26, 28, 30, 32, 34, 35, 37, 39, 41, 43, 45, 47, 49, 51, 52, 54, 56, 58, 60, 62, 64, 66, 68, 70, 72, 74, 76, 78, 80, 81, 83, 85, 87, 92, 94, 96, 98, 100, 102, 104, 106, 108, 110, 111, 114, 115, 118, 120, 121, 123, 125, 127, 129, 131, 133, 135, 137, 139, 144, 146, 148, 150, 152, 154, 156, 158, 160, 162, 164, 166, 168, 170, 175, 177, 179, 181, 183, 185, 187, 189, 190, 192, 194, 196, 198, 200, 202, 204, 206, 208, 210, 212, 214, 216, 218, 220, 222, 224, 225, 227, 229, 231, 233, 235, 237, 239, 241, 243, 245, 247, 249, 254, 257, 259, 261, 263, 265, 267, 269, 271, 273, 275, 277, 279, 281, 283, 285, 287, 289, 292, 294, 296, 298, 300, 302, 304, 306, 308, 310, 312, 314, 316, 318, 320, 322, 324, 326, 328, 330, 332, 334, 339, 341, 343, 345, 347, 349, 351, 353, 355, 357, 359, 361, 363, 365, 367, 370, 371, 373, 375, 377, 379, 381, 383, 385, 387, 389, 391, 393, 395, 397, 399, 401, 403, 405, 407, 409, 412, 414, 416, 418, 423, 425, 427, 429, 431, 433, 435, 437, 439, 441, 443, 445, 447, 449, 451, 453, 455, 457, 459, 461, 463, 465, 467, 469, 471, 474, 477, 479, 481,

CreativCare Learning Guides

483, 485, 487, 489, 491, 493, 495, 497, 499, 501, 503

Gross Motor, 7, 43, 45, 47, 49, 51, 52, 54, 56, 72, 96, 98, 104, 121, 123, 125, 127, 129, 131, 133, 135, 206, 208, 210, 212, 214, 216, 218, 220, 287, 289, 292, 294, 296, 298, 300, 302, 371, 372, 375, 377, 379, 381, 383, 385, 455, 457, 459, 461, 463, 465, 467, 469

I

Implementation, 13, 15, 17, 19, 21, 23, 25, 26, 28, 30, 32, 34, 35, 37, 39, 41, 43, 45, 47, 49, 51, 52, 54, 56, 58, 60, 62, 64, 66, 68, 70, 72, 74, 76, 78, 80, 81, 83, 85, 87, 92, 94, 96, 98, 100, 102, 104, 106, 108, 110, 112, 114, 116, 118, 120, 122, 124, 126, 128, 130, 132, 134, 136, 138, 140, 144, 146, 148, 150, 152, 154, 156, 158, 160, 162, 164, 166, 168, 170, 175, 177, 179, 181, 183, 185, 187, 189, 190, 192, 194, 196, 198, 200, 202, 204, 206, 208, 210, 212, 214, 216, 218, 220, 222, 224, 225, 227, 229, 231, 233, 235, 237, 239, 241, 243, 245, 247, 249, 254, 257, 259, 261, 263, 265, 267, 269, 271, 273, 275, 277, 279, 281, 283, 285, 287, 289, 292, 294, 296, 298, 300, 302, 304, 306, 308, 310, 312, 314, 316, 318, 320, 322, 324, 326, 328, 330, 332, 334, 339, 341, 343, 345, 347, 349, 351, 353, 355, 357, 359, 361, 363, 365, 367, 370, 371, 373, 375, 377, 379, 381, 383, 385, 387, 389, 391, 393, 395, 397, 399, 401, 403, 405, 407, 409, 412, 414, 416, 418, 423, 425, 427, 429, 431, 433, 435, 437, 439, 441, 443, 445, 447, 449, 451, 453, 455, 457, 459, 461, 463, 465, 467, 469, 471, 474, 477, 479, 481, 483, 485, 487, 489, 491, 493, 495, 497, 499, 501, 503

J

jump, 220, 294, 297, 373, 374, 382, 383, 386, 392, 463, 464, 469, 470

K

key concepts, 505, 506

L

Language, 7, 11, 57, 58, 59, 60, 62, 64, 66, 68, 70, 72, 89, 90, 102, 137, 139, 144, 146, 148, 150, 152, 154, 172, 173, 198, 206, 237, 239, 241, 243, 245, 247, 249, 252, 269, 292, 296, 298, 302, 304, 306, 308, 310, 312, 313, 314, 316, 318, 337, 367, 387, 389, 391, 393, 395, 407, 409, 412, 421, 423, 433, 441, 443, 445, 447, 451, 453, 470, 471, 473, 474, 476, 477, 478, 479, 480, 481, 482, 483, 484, 485, 487

Learning Basket, 9, 92, 94, 106, 108, 110, 112, 114, 116, 118, 120, 124, 132, 138, 146, 158, 160, 175, 177, 190, 192, 194, 198, 200, 202, 204, 218, 254, 257, 259, 261, 271, 273, 275, 277, 279, 280, 281, 296, 306, 308, 310, 314, 318, 319, 328, 332, 334, 425, 427, 431, 433, 435, 437, 439, 441, 443, 445, 447, 449, 451, 453, 471, 474, 481, 483, 491, 493, 495, 497, 499, 503

letter, 190, 191, 247, 248, 249, 250, 310, 347, 368, 369, 435, 453, 454, 481, 482, 487, 488

M

Maria Montessori
  Montessori, 8, 9

Memory, *347, 351*

N

name, *12, 15, 23, 87, 91, 108, 146, 147, 148, 150, 151, 152, 153, 156, 157, 159, 165, 166, 167, 214, 237, 247, 248, 254, 258, 259, 274, 311, 315, 336, 337, 346, 347, 352, 365, 369, 405, 413, 416, 422, 441, 443, 444, 448, 450, 479, 480, 485*

O

one-step commands, *312*

P

paint, *200, 201, 264, 300, 301, 367, 368, 369, 370, 449, 450, 452*
patterns, *114, 115, 339, 422, 432*
Personal-Social, *7, 12, 74, 76, 78, 80, 81, 83, 85, 87, 91, 156, 158, 160, 162, 164, 166, 168, 170, 174, 222, 224, 225, 227, 229, 231, 233, 235, 253, 320, 322, 324, 326, 328, 330, 332, 334, 338, 365, 370, 397, 399, 401, 403, 405, 414, 416, 418, 422, 489, 491, 493, 495, 497, 499, 501, 503*
pictures, *60, 91, 102, 103, 108, 116, 150, 245, 246, 252, 261, 262, 269, 306, 310, 311, 314, 315, 318, 319, 322, 332, 333, 343, 344, 350, 365, 391, 392, 401, 405, 407, 408, 412, 413, 425, 427, 428, 431, 433, 434, 436, 444, 447, 454, 471, 472, 473, 474, 481, 482, 497, 498*
play date, *225, 326, 327*
Play Dough, *279, 280*
pretend, *26, 155, 174, 214, 225, 231, 233, 329, 334, 335, 377, 381, 382, 403, 404, 416, 417*

problem-solve, *176, 297*
Pull Toy, *298*
Puzzle, *192, 341, 416, 425*

R

rules, *245, 302, 303, 368, 407, 465, 501, 502*

S

SAFETY, *294*
Sand, *370*
Scissors, *261, 349, 401, 447, 453*
sequence, *319, 338, 344, 373, 487*
Shapes, *192, 254, 345*
sign language, *140*
singing, *42, 52, 154, 165, 283, 382, 409, 420*
social interaction, *227, 505*
stuffed animal, *23, 43, 119, 179, 181, 189, 206, 212, 235, 308, 377, 401*
supplies, *118, 265, 339, 351, 363, 385, 427, 431, 433, 441, 443, 475, 483*

T

textures, *90, 114, 116, 124, 132, 339, 360*
toddler, *237, 238, 292, 296, 304, 305, 306, 307, 308, 309, 310, 311, 312, 314, 315, 316, 317, 318, 319, 320, 321, 322, 326, 332, 333, 459*
Toothbrush, *320*
two step commands, *312*

V

venues, *505*

CreativCare Learning Guides

W

Walk, 28, 63, 64, 78, 85, 98, 104, 221, 237, 381, 416, 440

Wash Your Hands, 322
water, 161, 229, 230, 279, 320, 323, 328, 329, 424, 497
work station, 505

Resources

Center, N. A. (2010). *Toddlers B; Language, social and Practical Life Activities for Children from 12 to 24 months.* North American Montessori Center.

Cherry, K. (2013). *About.com Psychology.* Retrieved 2013, from About.com: http://psychology.about.com/od/developmentalpsychology/a/childdevtheory.htm

Early Intervention Support. (n.d.). *Child Development Fine Motor Skills.* Retrieved from Early Intervention Support: http://www.earlyinterventionsupport.com/development/finemotor/3-6months.aspx

Education.com. (2013). *Preschool Worksheets.* Retrieved from Education.com: http://www.education.com/worksheets/preschool/

Excelligence Learning Corporation. (2012). *Early Childhood News.* Retrieved from Different Approaches to Teaching: Comparing Three Preschool Programs: http://www.earlychildhoodnews.com

Holland, L. (2012). *Growing Child.* Growing child.

Intervention, E. (2012). *How Children Develop.* Retrieved from Early Intervention.com: http://www.earlyinterventionsupport.com/

Jane Squires, P. D. (2009). Ages and Stages Questionnaire; Social-Emotional. Brookes Publishing Company.

Materials, D. D. (2011). Denver II Developmental Manual and Test Forms. Denver Developmental Materials.

Mcdevitt, T. M. (2013). *Child Development and Education.* Pearson.

Miller, K. (1994). *Things to Do with Toddlers and Twos.* Telshare Publishing.

Mooney, C. G. (2000). *Theories of Childhood; An Introduction to Dewey, Montessori, Erikson, Piaget and Vygotsky.* St. Paul: Redleaf Press.

Mullen, E. M. (1995). Mullens Scales of Early Learning. Circle Pines, Minnesota: American Guidance Services.

Newborg, J. (2005). Battelle Developmental Inventory; 2nd Edition. The Riverside Publishing Company.

PBS. (2012). *The Whole Child.* Retrieved from The ABC's Of Child Development: http://www.pbs.org/wholechild/abc/index.html

Pediatrics, A. A. (2009). *Caring for Your Baby and Young Child Birth to Age Five.* Bantum.

Silberg, J. (2002). *Games to Play with Toddlers, Revised* . Mt. Rainer: Gryphon House.

T. Berry Brazelton, M. J. (2002). *Touchpoints Birth to Three, Second Edition.* Da Capo Press.